HOSPICE
RESOURCE MANUAL
FOR
LOCAL CHURCHES

This book is designed for local churches, pastors, laypeople, interested citizens, hospice program administrators, and other health care leaders who desire to:

1. Study the caregiving needs of current and prospective terminally ill patients and families in the community.

2. Analyze the hospice programs in their area, and the problems they face, in order to be of constructive help in facilitating the best possible hospice care.

3. Involve churches in hospice care and support.

4. Educate the church constituency regarding hospice, and dying and death issues.

5. Understand aspects of spiritual pain, loss, and response in order to deepen ministry to people long before the advent of terminal illness.

6. Take leadership in assuring the future of hospice care by projecting appropriate state and national goals for hospice, including needed legislation; by motivating the corporate community, including the insurance industry, to act; and by developing adequate financial reimbursement.

HOSPICE RESOURCE MANUAL FOR LOCAL CHURCHES

Edited by JOHN W. ABBOTT

THE PILGRIM PRESS   NEW YORK

The biblical quotations, unless otherwise marked, are from the *Revised Standard Version of the Bible*, copyright 1946, 1952, and © 1971, 1973 by the Division of Christian Education, National Council of Churches, and are used by permission. The excerpts marked NEB are from *The New English Bible*. © The Delegates of the Oxford University Press and the Syndics of the Cambridge University Press, 1961, 1970. Used by permission.

Library of Congress Cataloging-in-Publication Data

Hospice resource manual for local churches.

   Bibliography: p. 85.
   1. Church work with the terminally ill.   2. Hospices (Terminal care).   3. Bereavement—Religious aspects—Christianity.   I. Abbott, John W., 1922–
BV4460.6.H67   1988   259′.4   87-29240
ISBN 0-8298-0763-2 (pbk.)

The Pilgrim Press, 132 West 31 Street, New York, NY 10001

Contents

Preface

The United Church Board for Homeland Ministries has been actively promoting the hospice movement in the United States since the early 1970s. In large part this resource manual is a legacy of the inspiration and persistent work of Helen Webber, former General Secretary of the Division for Health and Welfare, UCBHM. Before her retirement she identified the need for a resource guide to aid congregations in becoming actively involved in hospice ministries. The church and society owe her a large debt of gratitude.

It is with deep satisfaction that the UCBHM shares this work with the broader community in the hope that it will spread the hospice movement into yet unreached communities.

CHARLES SHELBY ROOKS
Executive Vice President
United Church Board for Homeland Ministries

Acknowledgments

For a decade I have seen firsthand the love, compassion, and concern for patients and their families demonstrated by the paid and volunteer staff of The Connecticut Hospice and its Institute for Education, Training, and Research. That experience has made this manual possible. In particular I acknowledge the invaluable counsel of Rosemary J. Hurzeler, whose distinguished leadership as President of both organizations has inspired leaders in many walks of life to keep the flame of hospice quality burning throughout America.

I acknowledge with gratitude and appreciation all of those whose writings are included herein with by-lines. Beth Polio originally wrote material that is included in chapters 10, 11, and 13. The following members of The Connecticut Hospice family assisted me with this project: Bess Bailey, Director of Support Services; Karen Burrows, Administrative Assistant; Lucile Hutchinson, Bereavement Team member; Muriel Kay, family member; Ellen Kessner, Director, The Connecticut Hospice Institute; Gayle Kimball, Director of Development and Community Relations; Ronnie Knight, Director, Budget and Reimbursement; Betsey Lewis, Education Specialist; Carl Osier, M.D., Staff Physician; and Robert P. Zanes, M.D., then Vice-President for Medical Affairs.

Throughout the process, the advice and counsel of James A. McDaniel, Secretary for Health and Welfare, United Church Board for Homeland Ministries, have been the essential ingredient without which the project could not have unfolded.

Thanks also goes to Michele Sebti, who typed the manuscript.

JOHN W. ABBOTT

Introduction

In early 1974 a cancer patient in New Haven, Connecticut, received a visitor. "I am here representing "Hospice," the visitor said, "and I've come to find out how we can help you." It was a foresighted question, heralding the start of a movement new to the United States, one based on the needs not only of patients, but of their families as well. And it was a program destined to ask many questions, and to formulate answers with the patients and their families as teachers and with professional and volunteer caregivers as willing students in a quest for a humanitarian approach to dying and family support.

Hospice care had originally been developed in England. Cicely Saunders, a nurse-turned-social worker-turned-physician played a pivotal role. Under her leadership, St. Christopher's Hospice opened in London in 1967. Dr. Saunders had visited New Haven, Connecticut, at the invitation of faculty and students of the Yale University School of Medicine in 1963 and had returned to New Haven again in 1967 to lecture at the Yale School of Nursing at the invitation of then Dean Florence Wald. After an interdisciplinary study of patient and family needs, The Connecticut Hospice was born in 1971 and sent its nursing director on her first home care visit, mentioned earlier, in 1974.

What has been the result of the hospice experience? It has clearly made major contributions to health care. From a consumer perspective, it has involved the family in the caregiving process, eased suffering and discomfort through the development of expertise in pain and symptom management, and created a new dimension of bereavement care after the death of the patient. As far as caregivers are concerned, hospice has demonstrated the viability and effectiveness of the interdisciplinary team.

Beyond that, hospice has reaffirmed the sacredness of human life through emphasis on quality of life for as long as life lasts. Such a notable achievement is a subtle thing, a matter of nuances, an affirmation that at times little things are more important than seemingly greater things. How people feel about the latter part of everyone's journey from birth to death *is* of tremendous importance. From the point of view of the patient, the fear of pain and discomfort has been dealt with in such a way as to provide freedom from at least some of the burdens of the illness in order to have the opportunity for additional fullness of life.

Hospice care is inevitably set over against the traditional health care system. Whereas the traditional system is designed to cure the patient, hospice care proclaims the principle of palliation: that at a particular phase of an illness, quality of life, made possible by comfort, is more important than longevity. Whereas the traditional system concentrates on the patient, hospice care encompasses the family. Whereas the traditional system has designed rules and regulations as a means of carrying on its role, hospice care de-emphasizes the rules, saying, for example, that in an inpatient setting, family members of any age should be allowed to visit at any hour of the day or night.

All this is of tremendous concern to local church parishes. The Body of Christ at the local level consists of people, and with the rapidly increasing longevity of the population, more and more people are dying of cancer, AIDS, and other forms of terminal illness. What is the response of the community of faith to these needs?

Hospice care represents unique combinations of approaches that have always been part and parcel of the caring functions of the local church. Hospice care is old, in that it returns to families certain roles that technological health care had taken away from them. Yet hospice is new, in terms of what it says about dying and about living fully for as long as life lasts.

To the church, which focuses much of its activity on the homes of the members of its flock, the fact that in hospice, the family is the unit of care is a vivid demonstration of a philosophy of community life and parish living. And it is an approach to life strongly centered in medicine and dependent on nursing as a profession.

Hospice care is professional in terms of the caliber and skills of those needed to provide care, but volunteers are also intrinsic to hospice and in fact have found in hospice a status and purpose seldom granted to the unpaid in an era of organizational specialization and professionalism.

And hospice is a grass-roots response to the needs of people, and was picked up and facilitated in countless numbers of local communities. Yet it is now a widespread phenomenon and has achieved geographical diversity in a national sense.

The hospice movement has spread rapidly since the first patient was cared for in 1974. In 1986 the National Hospice Organization (NHO) identified 1,568 hospice programs, of which 103 were in the planning stages. The geographical extent of the movement is indicated by the following breakdown of statistics from more than 1,400 such programs that replied to the NHO survey.

Alabama	16	Kentucky	24	Ohio	51
Alaska	4	Louisiana	14	Oklahoma	15
Arizona	14	Maine	27	Oregon	32
Arkansas	9	Maryland	34	Pennsylvania	81
California	133	Massachusetts	53	Puerto Rico	1
Colorado	24	Michigan	77	Rhode Island	5
Connecticut	26	Minnesota	52	South Carolina	11
Delaware	4	Mississippi	8	South Dakota	10
District of					
Columbia	3	Missouri	24	Tennessee	24
Florida	32	Montana	17	Texas	36
Georgia	24	Nebraska	17	Utah	10
Hawaii	8	Nevada	5	Vermont	13
Idaho	14	New Hampshire	25	Virginia	33
Illinois	59	New Jersey	40	Washington	29
Indiana	30	New Mexico	9	West Virginia	11
Iowa	36	New York	46	Wisconsin	41
Kansas	29	North Carolina	55	Wyoming	6
		North Dakota	5		

Hospice availability, it will be noted, is widely scattered throughout the country. Programs in small towns or rural areas tend to deliver hospice services differently from those in cities. Accessibility to hospices is therefore a primary topic for consideration in the parish context, and the factors leading to the presence or absence of hospice care need to be analyzed.

WHAT DOES "HOSPICE" MEAN?

Throughout the United States there are multiple types of care offered to patients and families under the hospice name. For purposes of this guide, "hospice" is defined as an interdisciplinary program of care for terminally ill patients and their families that emphasizes quality of life for the patient and supportive help for the family during the time of illness and the bereavement period. Hospice care is medically directed and nurse-coordinated, and encompasses the disciplines of social work, pastoral care, pharmacology, the arts, and the services of volunteers professionally trained for their work. Hospice care is palliative rather than curative, and stresses pain and symptom management designed for the patient's comfort. Hospice care represents a continuum centered wherever appropriate in the home and based on the availability of twenty-four-hours-a-day, seven-days-a-week on-call home visits from competent professionals. Suitable arrangements for inpatient care are essential when home care is inappropriate or when the needs of the patient and family can be better served in a special hospice environment.

STANDARDS

Another factor compounding the difficulty from both a consumer and a hospice perspective is that there is no nationally agreed-upon definition of services implied by the name hospice. Legislation establishing the Hospice Medicare Benefit does define certain minimal requirements for certification of the hospice program as one in which Medicare-eligible patients may receive benefits. However, only 275 out of 1,568 hospices have become certified as of mid-1986.

The Joint Commission on the Accreditation of Hospitals (JCAH) has adopted hospice standards.

Although any hospice may seek accreditation, JCAH approval is required only for hospital-based hospices.

STATE REGULATIONS

Some states have adopted statewide hospice licensure or other regulatory standards. But there is a vast difference between definitions and requirements for caregiving. Whether or not state regulations have "teeth" in them is, for example, a valid question for exploration. One needs to ask at every point exactly what patients and families may expect and what kinds of care are offered. In home care programs who makes home visits? What are the credentials and qualifications of the caregivers?

LEVEL OF CARE

Is the level of care sufficient to deal with the sickness of the patients during the latter part of their lives? Chapter 3 will help with the determination of what patients are appropriate for hospice care and at what point in the illness.

One analysis of hospice inpatients (carried on in The Connecticut Hospice) placed them in the 90th percentile of the Case Mix Index, which describes the number of multiple factors that are present in an illness. The comparison was made between that organization's inpatient building and 7,000 acute care hospitals throughout the country.

MINORITY CONCERNS

Yet another issue has to do with ethnic and racial inclusiveness of hospice care throughout the United States. The fact is that there is relatively little minority involvement within American hospice programs. Some of the factors that are part of this situation are analyzed on pages 11–12.

WHAT IS THE FUTURE OF HOSPICE CARE?

The introductory years of hospice care in the United States represent only the beginning. What is the place of hospice care within our national goals? What new frontiers of hospice care await attention and development in the community? What additional steps will be taken to improve coverage of the costs of care? And, especially, what is the church's role in the next decade of hospice? What is the local congregation's response to hospice care?

1

THE LOCAL CHURCH— A COURSE OF ACTION

Hospice care is too new to survive without a struggle. The local church is intrinsically suited to participate in that struggle.

The local congregation is a community, its members united in commitment to God through Christ and bound to one another by unique ties. The relationship within the local church began in the upper room, continues through the Lord's Supper, and is refined from day to day by the networks of interrelationships that cross generational lines. Such networks—reflected both in formal organizational ways and through informal chains of human contact—constantly relate those within the church to acute needs that arise. The approach of death is one of those needs.

No one should die alone. Every dying human being is part of a family of greater or lesser proportions, and the family is affected in countless ways by the death of one of its members. The church is also part of the dying process because it is bound with its members on their journey through life.

In an informal sense, the numerous networks within the parish are a major factor in the support systems that the church encompasses for its people. But the congregation bears a corporate responsibility as well. The church is responsible for *whether* its members are prepared to die and for *how* they die. The church is responsible for any degree of spiritual pain felt by those who are part of its family. The church cares for its own people, and for those within the geographical community who, although not officially on the rolls, are nonetheless a concern of its outreach.

The family of which the dying person is a part is innately of the parish also, and the way in which bereavement needs are met says much about the way the church relates to its own people.

HOW CAN THE LOCAL CHURCH DEAL WITH HOSPICE ISSUES? THE PROCESS

The material included in this manual lends itself to a participatory process that cuts across a variety of age levels within the church. At the center of the process an existing board or committee could spearhead the effort, or a separate representative committee could be brought together for this purpose.

Depending on its interest, a congregation may work to a greater or lesser degree on the problem. Such varying patterns may be categorized as "levels" of activity. Such levels are shown by the following.

1

Level 1. Be aware of the acknowledged existence of one or more hospice programs in the community or area, and work with them in appropriate ways, such as referring patients and families, encouraging church members to volunteer, visiting if there is a place for inpatient care.

Level 2. Appoint a group to make a complete study of what care for the terminally ill and their families is available in the area. Assess the needs of prospective patients in both the parish and the community at large. Study questions of financial reimbursement and develop action plans to stimulate further coverage. Such a study could include the holding of weeknight or Sunday forums with guest speakers and the formulation of recommendations for extension of what is now available.

Level 3. Become an ardent advocate for hospice care by pursuing every possible avenue, including the exploration of parish sponsorship of a hospice program either individually or in coalition with other groups. A decision to sponsor hospice should not be taken lightly, for the study will uncover some of the tremendous complexities of the subject.

In any individual situation it may be desirable to pursue combinations of levels. Regardless of the extent of participation as the process begins, there are several major perspectives with which the problems will be approached. These are demonstrated in the following list:

Congregational Perspectives in Hospice Care

Pastoral care perspectives.
• Who are the people who need or are likely to need care?

What are their needs?
• Are there currently referrals that need to be made?

What is the church's responsibility in this regard?
• In order to make hospice care effective, are there ways in which the church should help? Are there people who could remain at home rather than be institutionalized if the church assumed a "pri-

mary" care responsibility for them? In this category are there single people and those who are elderly or incapacitated?
• What is the relationship of the church to other community organizations, such as home care agencies and private duty nursing agencies?

Clergy perspectives.
• What is the opportunity for pastoral participation in the interdisciplinary team process? How can the church best maintain a sense of presence?
• Does related seminary curriculum adequately prepare for caring for the dying? for family support?
• What educational process needs to be carried out in the parish regarding death? (see below)

The perspective of hospice needs.
• Is the church a center for the recruitment of volunteers to work in the hospice program?
• Does the church assist in any way with efforts to secure financial support?
• Are opportunities provided for hospice speakers before the congregation or various of its groups?
• Does the church consider that it has a responsibility to assist with orientation and training of professionals or volunteers in the community to meet hospice needs? (The Checklist for Consumers, prepared by the National Consumers League, offers a helpful basis for exploring the hospice situation. See page 89.)

The congregation in bereavement.
• How can the local congregation best take care of the bereavement needs of its members? What can it do to facilitate the hospice bereavement program? Are there principles that could be applied in the church to other bereavement needs, including sudden deaths, as well?

Referral timing.
• What is the appropriate time for referral of patients to hospice programs?

Understanding of death.
• Would the congregation be enriched by an educational effort to discuss, interpret, and understand death? In general, are attitudes good, or is the subject ignored?

FURTHER DEFINING THE CHURCH ROLE

If there is no hospice program in the community, or if such coverage appears to be inadequate, a congregation would be well advised to work with other churches and with the existing health care community in seeking to establish such a program. Hospice administrative issues are so complex that if a single parish were to set up and establish such a program, the resulting situation could well drain a tremendous amount of energy from other interests of the church. But several churches working ecumenically could stimulate development of a program; hospitals, home health agencies, health care planning agencies, and others could be helpful in the process.

Likewise, the congregation would do well to define part of its role as stimulating others to work on behalf of patients and their families, rather than attempting to do the job itself. For example, in the highly important field of research, encouraging university-based research staffs to work on hospice issues would be wiser than attempting to carry on a church-based research effort.

2

BIBLICAL AND THEOLOGICAL BASIS FOR HOSPICE

*Edward M. Huenemann**

His love was his death. . . . I didn't know how much I loved him until he was gone. Is love like that?

—*Nicholas Wolterstorff†*

In the final moment Jesus said, "Father into your hands I commit my spirit." Death is the holy boundary to life beyond which we can reach only by faith. All other boundaries that we cross on the path of life are minor or major risks, ventures of faith, on the road to meaning and fulfillment. But death is the ultimate boundary we cross and can accept only as an act of final commitment to God, the source of life itself.

Jesus' final commitment to God was the same commitment by which he lived all his life. He always lived beyond known boundaries, and by faith and trust offered himself to the unknown, the stranger, the world in a breadth and depth of love so meaningful that those who knew him called him the son of God. His life and death became to them the way of salvation. They identified with him, and in his name they, too, began to live and die. In him they tasted the power of life beyond death. In him they both knew and accepted their mortality but

lived for purposes beyond their own limits and interests to the glory of God. Into God's hands they committed *their* spirits.

Dietrich Bonhoeffer, the noted twentieth-century theologian and martyr under Hitler, observed on the way to his own death, "For you this is the end, but for me the beginning of life." Our life history is our boundary, but the source of our life lies beyond it, in God. The Bible and Christian tradition, therefore, speak not simply of the immortality of the soul, but of death and resurrection. We are always moving toward death, but our "thousand deaths" are not the last word. We live by the power of eternal life, by resurrection. The logic of death is forever overcome by the miraculous power of resurrection and life. Death is real, but life is victorious.

Christian life, therefore, does not deny the reality of either death or the sins and evil attendant on the fear of it. Christian faith recognizes "the last enemy" but knows that not the last enemy, but our ultimate friend has the final word. Christian life is therefore a life of devotion and struggle. It is life devoted to what the well-known Swiss theologian Karl Barth called "the continuum of the divine consummation."‡ In more common terminology, it is

---

*Director of Theology in Global Context Association.

†*Lament for a Son* (Grand Rapids, MI: William B. Eerdmans, 1987), pp. 12–13.

‡Karl Barth, *Credo* (New York: Charles Scribner's Sons, 1962), p. 203.

life devoted to the life and eternal purpose of God who loves us. It is life lived by faith that reaches beyond death and evil, not only while we escape these evils, but even while we pass through them, even unknowingly or unconsciously.

The devout believer neither denies death or its powers, nor simply seeks escape. The devout believer fights for life, even in his or her dying. Jesus himself both resisted death and accepted it. He resisted the powers that sought to impose it but accepted it, and even willingly offered his life to God. He prayed that if it were possible, "this cup" should pass from him, yet "not my will, but thy will be done." In that paradox, in that struggle, faith seeks life, and devotion finds expression.

So to talk about death and dying is but the traditional and theological way of trying to express the mystery that surrounds it. Even the Bible does not try to explain the incomprehensible, but it does bear faithful witness both to its power and essential evil and to the hope and faith by which it is overcome.

Our own era and culture speak of it quite differently. In the Bible and Christian tradition, life comes from God and returns to God, and both birth and death are mysteries beyond analysis. In today's world, life has become more self-centered and biologically focused and defined. Society is struggling for precise definitions of the beginning and end of life in biological terms in the hope that clarity can be achieved on such issues as abortion and euthanasia. The discussion, while inevitable and necessary for clarification of ethical behavior, may or may not contribute to our ability to deal with life and death. Our capacity to deal with them is not based on technique, or biological precision, but on faith, hope, and love. Technical precision can help us focus our effort toward more adequate expressions of faith, hope, and love in the face of death, but biological technique cannot substitute for them.

Ministry and support of life in the presence of death are, therefore, immediate and urgent issues. The biological focus of our culture has made us appreciate the significance of the body and the realities of our physical existence. But the goodness of life is not identical with a strong, beautiful, healthy, even sexy body. Any handicap, deformity, or bodily limitation is too readily understood only as a distraction and limitation on life itself. That real fulfillment of life lies beyond bodily limitation is not realized, and that human life is realized in the spirit is overlooked. The real promise in life is missed. Our lives are reduced to that of healthy animals. Concern for the preservation of the body takes precedence over the growth and victory of the spirit.

This failure to focus on the nurture of the spirit is evidence that the Christian faith is not taken seriously. The apostle Paul puts the issue bluntly. "If the dead are never raised to life, 'let us eat and drink, for tomorrow we die'" [1 Cor. 15:32, NEB]. If there is nothing beyond the preservation of our bodies, if life is not centered in the human spirit, then eating and drinking and care for the body are adequate. But we are not so constituted. Human life is lived in the body but focused beyond the body. Its fullness and meaning require more.

For the apostle, as for all Christians, the central focus is the resurrection. Our bodies, like seeds planted in the ground, are subjected to disintegration and death, but the glory, meaning, and fullness of our lives appear not in disintegration, but in the life revealed beyond it—in the resurrection (1 Corinthians 15:35–44). God's own interest in our lives becomes evident beyond the boundary of death even as God's own interest in and love of Jesus became evident after his death through the resurrection. It is Christ's appearances to his disciples after his death that revealed his true life in God and his full glory. Only then did it become apparent that the life of Jesus was much more than a matter of eating and drinking until death overtook him. Jesus' life in the flesh was a constant pursuit of that newness of life in God that we approach only as we offer our own bodies as living sacrifices, which is a "reasonable service" (Romans 12:1–2). The promise hidden in Christ's resurrection is what programs our lives as believers. It gives them focus and centers them on the meaning and fulfillment that God wills for them. In that promise rests the power to accept death without being its victim. Death is the last enemy to be overcome.

It is helpful to note that not only the apostle Paul, but also the whole biblical record assumes that life can be, and often is, focused differently. The apostle and other biblical writers linked sin and death. Paul writes: "If the dead are never raised to life, 'let us eat and drink, for tomorrow we die.'" But then he adds, "Make no mistake: 'Bad company is the ruin of a good character.' Come back to a sober and upright life and leave your sinful ways. There are some who know nothing of God; to your shame I say it" [1 Cor. 15:32–34, NEB]. The apostle was aware that a person who loses his or her awareness of God's own interest in his or her life, the promise of the resurrection, loses the spiritual connection that is essential to his or her being in God.

"As in Adam all men die, so in Christ all will be brought to life" [1 Cor. 15:22, NEB]. Adam attempted to live the self-centered life that separated itself from its source in God and so had no goal but death. Sin and death thus entered the heart of human experience. That wounding of the human soul is every person's pain and cannot be ignored. The church used to speak of the "cure of souls." Our biologically focused age has all but ignored the need of it. People are submitted to hospitals as though they were being placed in a body repair shop. There they can be left to die like Adam. Their self-centered life reaches its end, and the fullness of its meaning and glory goes uncelebrated. Death gets the last word. The eating and drinking process simply ends.

Apparently the apostle believed that such a dismal attitude about life can become pervasive and warned his readers about it. "Make no mistake: 'Bad company is the ruin of a good character.'" People can be seduced into self-centered living that has no other end than self-centered and lonely death. Both body and soul can perish in meaninglessness.

It is the glory of the "New Adam," of Christ, that he engaged vigorously in the "cure of souls." As the "great physician" he not only healed bodies, but also nourished human spirits when he offered his own body for others in a bond of love so profound that not death, but he has the last word. He discredited Adam's self-centered life and restored human living to its union with God and one another. Through him the full promise of life was restored. Death is no longer the loss of one's center, but the discovery of one's center in God—in life's source. "God is not only the God of the sufferers but the God who suffers. The pain and fallenness of humanity have entered into his heart. Through the prism of my tears I have seen a suffering God."*

This theological drama at the depth of human life is often ignored in our "secular" age. Neither "sin" nor "death" is a permissible topic for discussion in polite society. Nor is the "cure of souls" seen as a necessary function in a consumer society in which every human need can be met by pur-

chase except the need for life itself and the love of it. We are in "bad company" that threatens our "character." The fact that our human destiny is not a significant consideration in our life-style only means that those touched by deeper human sensibility need to break the pattern of insensitivity and serve the "great physician" in the "cure of souls." There is more to living and dying than our society dreams of.

> God is love. That is why he suffers. To love our suffering sinful world is to suffer. God so suffered for the world that he gave up his only Son to suffering. The one who does not see God's suffering does not see his love. God is suffering love.†

LIFE WITH THE DYING

I have looked at death and dying in theological perspective. I have looked at biblical references to them and have sought to highlight certain dogmatic assumptions on which the Christian faith rests its perspective. I briefly summarize these assumptions here as the basis for further ethical and behavioral considerations.

1. Human life has a theocentric focus. From beginning to end it is a gift of God. We exist, therefore, as *response-able* creatures, and in that response-ability our fulfillment rests.
2. We exist in bodies, but our bodies are not the limit of our existence. Faith, hope, and love are ways of reaching beyond our bodily confines.
3. Self-centeredness, the fall into sin, restricts our lives to the bodily boundary of death and keeps us from transcending ourselves to discover the fulfillment and joy that become real in commitment to God. Sin and death are our ultimate enemies.
4. The resurrection of Jesus, his living power and appearance to his disciples after his crucifixion, is the basis of our hope in the promise of resurrection and eternal life. God reaches out to us across the divide of sin and death and awaits our return to God.

These are key dogmatic assumptions, drawn from the biblical story, that shape the Christian's

*Wolterstorff, *Lament for a Son*, p. 81.

†Ibid., p. 90.

understanding. But a secular and scientific age like ours regards such understanding as "mythical," and therefore not useful for practical guidance in life. In that way our theological and religious assumptions get separated from our ethical and practical decisions, and our religious life and common daily life run on separate tracks.

It is precisely in the face of death that this kind of dualistic existence collapses and the sharp line between the "mythical" and the "scientific" cannot be maintained. Concerns for meaning, fulfillment, and evaluation become primary. But such concerns reach beyond physical and even scientific limits to the dimensions of the spirit. They find their deepest expression in precisely the kind of language of story and poetry that we too easily dismiss as "mythical." It is, however, just such "mythical" language that is essential for the expression of the deepest and most fundamental dimensions of the human experience. Their very depth and significance defy the boundaries of "scientific" categorization. Love, for example, is a profound reality in human life, but without metaphysical, mythical, or poetic language its reality cannot be grasped.

So the ultimate depth of life and death cannot be approached except by an appreciation for the assumptions of faith in the "mythological," religious, and poetic language in which those assumptions find expression. Ministry and service with and to the dying is therefore much more than a "scientific" venture, although it is that as regards basic care for the body. Ministry and service are *primarily* arts. They require sensitivity to those dimensions of human experience that have shaped the assumptions or "dogmas" of theological insight as it emerges at the ultimate center of human existence. This means dealing with peoples' faith, hope, and love, or lack thereof, in an intelligent way much beyond the limits of physical or scientific "fact." Spiritual wisdom is essential to the art of ministry with and to the dying.

This implies that a Christian engaged in such ministry allows the assumptions summarized above to serve as guides of understanding in his or her ministry with or to the dying. Life for both the patient and the minister has theocentric focus. We both and together seek, therefore, to exercise our *response-ability* to God and to each other. Together we approach the boundary of life as an encounter with the source of all life—God. It is a "holy hour" in which we trust not simply what we know, but the One by whom we are known. It is a time of profound commitment. Anything less denies the patient the dignity and respect due him or her. Whether prayer is made audible or not, no one should enter such holy hours without prayer in heart and mind.

We exist in bodies. This requires the closest possible attention to every bodily need the patient has. However, it would be a gross mistake to assume that that is all that is required of us in these late hours. Both the patient and I know that we live and have lived by faith, hope, and love. Our spirits hunger for them more than ever. They are legitimate subjects for discussion, for prayer, and especially for demonstration. Our ability to deal with them artfully may be limited. But it is not our skill, but the authenticity and honesty of the effort that will support both the patient and the servant in these crucial moments.

Self-centeredness has afflicted us all. It is the sting of death. We have regrets and even degrees of feelings of guilt. Too often we have not transcended ourselves to join in the fullness of life with others, or creation, or God. We missed it and we know it. It does not help to hide the fact. Confession is good for the soul. Patient and attendant may both and together wish to be honest and open about our failures and even our "sin." The assurance of Jesus Christ that God is not the enemy, but the friend of sinners may well control our behavior. Self-righteous or judgmental attitudes have no place at the boundary of life with and in God. Our true center will remove all self-centered anguish from us.

The resurrection of Jesus is the sign given us for our future beyond the boundary of death. We cannot reach beyond that boundary. For us it is the end. Yet the spirit of Christ reaches out to us from the center of divine life, offering certain assurance that God is for us and not against us. Even in death God will not forsake us. Our life was not in vain. Its future and its fruit are in God's hands. Is that "myth," or is that "reality"? It is the basic reality of all life to which only "myth" or "metaphor" or "poetry" can speak, but we know it to be true. Our beginning was not in our own hands. Nor is our end. Ultimate reality is beyond us. That is what resurrection means. It is the promise of life beyond our own power. That is always true. Life is a mystery beyond our own power.

The drafters of the Westminster Confession asked, "What is the chief end of [persons]?" and answered, "To glorify God and enjoy [God] forever." There is nothing to say beyond that. But sober reflection must help us realize that there has never really been anything else really worth doing.

With assumptions like these in heart and mind the art of ministry with, to, and for the dying becomes a possibility. Not that these assumptions will tell us what to do or automatically provide the skills to do it. But without some such basic assumptions we will find it difficult to minister significantly no matter how skilled we may otherwise be. In fact, when these assumptions impact our hearts and minds, avenues of human relationship may open up between the patient and ourselves that will enable us to enter this holy ground together in faith, hope, and love. That is a gift to be sought from God.

CONCLUSION

Nothing written in these paragraphs should be understood to imply that any skills, techniques, or scientific methods and aids should be neglected by either the patient or the person helping the patient. On the contrary, a basic theological perspective should prompt us to use such available tools as wisely and diligently as possible. But if we are not informed and disciplined by some such theological perspective, it is not likely that we will make wise use of the tools available to us.

The art of ministry with the dying is an exercise in wisdom and understanding so profound that it discloses to us our common humanity and gives birth to the newness of life that the future holds. When Jesus committed his spirit into the hands of God he revealed the secret of his life from the beginning. When Bonhoeffer said, "For you this is the end, for me the beginning of life" he knew the promise revealed in Jesus the Christ. Our own "end" teaches us that there is purpose to life and death—the glorification of God and enjoyment of life forever—even beyond death. There is more to it than selfish dreaming can teach us. Life is a gift from and to God, who puts us in touch with reality.

We're in it together, God and we, together in the history of our world. The history of our world is the history of our suffering together. Every act of evil extracts a tear from God, every plunge into anguish extracts a sob from God. But also the history of our world is the history of our deliverance together. God's work to release himself from his suffering is his work to deliver the world from its agony; our struggle for joy and justice is our struggle to relieve God's sorrow.

When God's cup of suffering is full, our world's redemption is fulfilled. Until justice and peace embrace, God's dance of joy is delayed.

The bells for the feast of divine joy are the bells for the shalom of the world.*

*Ibid., p. 91.

3

PATIENT AND FAMILY NEEDS ...AND HOSPICE RESPONSE

THE PREVALENCE OF CANCER

Although people who are dying from a number of different terminal illnesses are eligible for hospice care, the majority (90% to 95%) are cancer patients. The progression of cancer makes it easier to define the specific prognosis in terms of time, but as any physician will indicate, no one can tell for sure how long any patient is likely to live.

The American Cancer Society (ACS) estimates 73 million Americans who are currently living will develop cancer—about 30% of the population. Cancer will eventually strike in three out of four families.

Tremendous advances have been made in the treatment of cancer. Whereas in the 1930s fewer than 20% of cancer victims were alive five years after treatment, today the figure is 40%. And when figures such as a normal life expectancy are taken into consideration, the ACS reports that the true figure is 49%.

The ACS also projected that in 1986, 472,000 persons would die of cancer and that there would be 930,000 new cases. The death rate rises each year, largely because of the increasing longevity of the population.

INTERDISCIPLINARY TEAM

According to the hospice concept, the patient and family are surrounded by an interdisciplinary team. Each team member demonstrates a specific area of expertise and at the same time seeks to enhance the role of other team members. Looking at hospice from the outside, the practical workings of such a team are difficult to understand. Pastors and others who attempt to minister to hospice patients may experience a wide variance in the level of team functioning. In some instances those who call themselves a team may not truly function as one; in other cases, although the team members may have developed some understanding of how to work together, it may be difficult for outsiders (such as pastors) to become part of the deliberative process.

Because of financial considerations, all hospices do not always have a full complement of hospice disciplines available. At the same time the ideal of the team remains a constant challenge to all those seeking to be hospice advocates in order that the patients and families served may have a full measure of hospice quality of life open to them.

The hospice patient profile will help one to understand the particular characteristics of those who are being served. Each patient, however, possesses

Note Your State

What does this mean in terms of any specific state? The map below shows the distribution of new cancer cases for 1986.

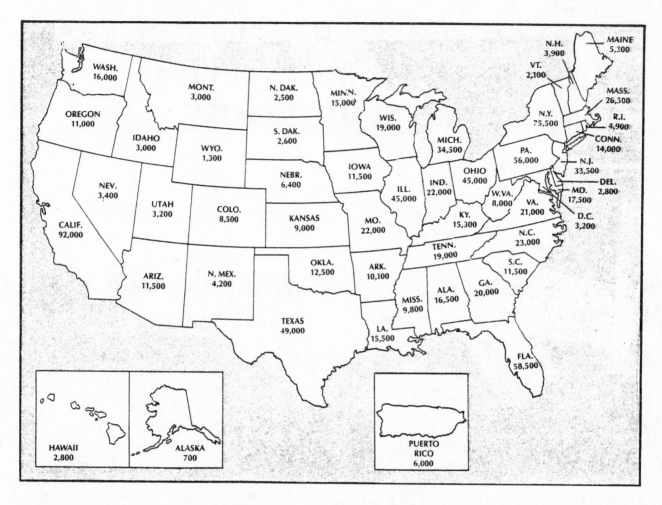

Estimated number of new cancer cases in 1986 by states, total: 930,000* (excluding Puerto Rico).
*Excluding non-melanoma skin cancer and carcinoma in situ. BASED ON RATES FROM NCI SEER PROGRAM (1977–1981).
Reproduced by permission of American Cancer Society® from *1986 Cancer Facts and Figures.*

Estimated cancer deaths for 1986 are cited in the following American Cancer Society tabulation, together with the death rate per 100,000 population.

STATE	NUMBER OF DEATHS	DEATH RATE PER 100,000 POPULATION
Alabama	8,300	203
Alaska	400	84
Arizona	5,800	165
Arkansas	5,200	211
California	47,000	180
Colorado	4,300	125
Connecticut	7,000	224
Delaware	1,400	227
District of Columbia	1,700	309
Florida	29,800	249
Georgia	10,000	169
Hawaii	1,400	130
Idaho	1,500	135
Illinois	23,500	205
Indiana	11,000	196
Iowa	6,000	203
Kansas	4,700	194
Kentucky	7,800	199
Louisiana	8,000	176
Maine	2,600	218
Maryland	9,000	205
Massachusetts	13,300	233
Michigan	17,600	188
Minnesota	7,600	179
Mississippi	4,800	180

STATE	NUMBER OF DEATHS	DEATH RATE PER 100,000 POPULATION
Missouri	11,100	221
Montana	1,500	176
Nebraska	3,300	205
Nevada	1,700	155
New Hampshire	2,000	189
New Jersey	17,000	228
New Mexico	2,000	138
New York	38,400	228
North Carolina	11,500	184
North Dakota	1,300	194
Ohio	23,200	215
Oklahoma	6,400	193
Oregon	5,300	173
Pennsylvania	28,400	241
Rhode Island	2,500	263
South Carolina	5,700	168
South Dakota	1,400	201
Tennessee	9,600	196
Texas	24,400	150
Utah	1,700	88
Vermont	1,100	200
Virginia	10,600	185
Washington	7,900	169
West Virginia	4,100	205
Wisconsin	9,500	193
Wyoming	700	114
United States	472,000	196
Puerto Rico	3,000	94

a unique individuality and no two patients are alike. Yet statistics indicate that most patients fall into certain categories.

The Connecticut Hospice, which operates both a home care program that serves an eighteen-town/city area and an inpatient service for the population of the entire state, tabulated the following patient profile for the 1985 fiscal year:

1,101 patients/families were served, 712 receiving inpatient care only, 193 receiving home care only, and 196 a combination of both.

Patient Population Profile by Percentage

AGE:	Under 65	28.1%	Over 65	71.9%
SEX:	Female	48.8%	Male	51.2%
RACE:	Black	5.5%	White	94.5%
MARITAL STATUS	Married	51.4%	Widowed	31.7%
	Single	9.0%	Divorced	6.6%
	Separated	1.3%		

Diagnosis: cancer in 90% of patients.

Length of Stay

The Connecticut Hospice has experienced a decline in the length of stay of its patients. The home care length of stay has decreased from an overall average of 48.07 days in 1984 to an estimated 35.34 days in 1986. The average inpatient length of stay went down from 17.85 days in 1984 to an estimated 14.45 days in 1986.

An important question for any hospice is whether patients are referred early enough to enable the patient and family to receive the full benefit of hospice attention. There also seems to be a correlation between the time of referral for hospice care and the introduction of the DRGs (diagnosis-related groups) into hospitals. In the DRG system, payment is made on the basis of an illness or procedure, regardless of how long the care may take. (See also pages 48–49.)

MINORITIES AND HOSPICE CARE

Although national figures are unavailable concerning minorities served through hospice programs, by and large hospices have done a better job of reaching a white middle-class population than they have of reaching racial or ethnic minorities.

When the problem is discussed, the following questions are raised in this regard: What is the effect of hospice emphasis on the need for a primary referring physician on populations in which a family doctor may not be the accepted norm? Are there ethnic variations in the way death or illness is met and handled by a family? If most hospice caregivers in a given community are Caucasian, how do people feel about being cared for exclusively by people of a different race?

Clearly hospices need to encourage research on these and related issues if hospice is to serve the entire population with equal effectiveness.

ALL-CHURCH EXERCISE

Patients and members of their families have *spoken* and *unspoken* needs. Spoken needs are those that people feel comfortable talking about; unspoken needs represent issues or questions that may not be discussed. For example, some kinds of cancer cause considerable disfigurement. The patient's feelings about the pain may be openly discussed, but his or her feelings about the alteration in body image may never be mentioned in conversations between the patient and family members.

The following topics represent categories of need; church groups will no doubt think of others:

Physical needs. Examples: pain resulting from surgery or tumor; nausea and vomiting; difficulty in eating; feelings of weakness or dizziness when the patient tries to walk.

Social needs. Why have one's friends stopped visiting? What is going on in the community, with a favorite team, etc.?

Economic needs. Paying hospital bills; loss of income; how the family will fare after death occurs.

Emotional needs. Inability to communicate with family members; depression, worry, fear, concern at what will happen; undue use of alcohol.

Spiritual needs. (See chapter 5 on Spiritual Pain.) What death means to the individual; relationship

with God; attitudes toward immortality; aspects of guilt and forgiveness.

The more the church congregation, at every level, "puts itself into the shoes" of patients and members of their families, the more there will be a general appreciation of hospice care.

There are, of course, many correlations with Quality of Life goals discussed in chapter 4, and these may also be discussed if desired.

PATIENT RIGHTS—FAMILY RIGHTS

The foundation of the hospice movement is a fundamental conviction of the importance of honoring the individual creed and philosophy of each patient and family unit served by the program. No person offering care has the right to superimpose his or her own philosophy on patients and their families.

Likewise, hospice care stresses the role of the family. The term significant other is often used to describe supportive roles in caregiving. The significant other for the patient may not be a legally married spouse; a couple may have been living together without being married. Or the patient may have had a homosexual liaison. In such cases it would be contrary to hospice experience and practice for those giving care to impose their own standards or expectations on the dying and the potentially grieving.

In addition to stressing the importance of patients and their families, there is also an implicit feeling about the importance of patient rights. *The Dying Person's "Bill of Rights"* of the Columbia-Montour Home Health Services, Inc., of Bloomsburg, Pennsylvania (below) presents this concern.

Sometimes the feelings that a patient has regarding his or her rights and those that family members have may be in conflict. The following illustrations demonstrate a few of the possible problems.

1. After many long and painful months of surgery, radiation, and chemotherapy, an elderly patient may have arrived at a desire for a palliative rather than a curative approach to cancer. From the patient's standpoint, the hospice alternative is meaningful and exciting, and the patient is achieving a genuine sense of personal fulfillment as death approaches. Then an absent relative arrives on

The Family Needs Chart is included in *A Guide for Developing a Hospice Orientation Program,* published by The Connecticut Hospice Institute. This exercise may be used with various age-groups within the parish. It may be copied on a chalkboard or duplicated for distribution.

FAMILY NEEDS CHART*

P = Patient   F = Family   P/F = Patient and Family

Needs	Physical	Social	Economic	Psychological	Spiritual
Spoken					
Unspoken					

*Reprinted by permission of The Connecticut Hospice Institute. Permission is hereby granted to local churches to duplicate the chart.

It will also be instructive to ask the group to discuss possible correlations between meeting the patient's family's needs and the patient's stage of illness when he or she is referred to the hospice program. The session leader may be interested in seeing how participants from a number of health care institutions filled out this chart (see below) during a pilot orientation program.

FAMILY NEEDS CHART

P = Patient   F = Family   P/F = Patient and Family

Needs	Physical	Social	Economic	Psychological	Spiritual
Spoken	Pain control P Stan: It seems to be harder to keep her comfortable. F	Will friends keep visiting? P Louise: I'm trying to balance school and the house and my brothers and my own life—too much. F	Mustn't let patient know of financial problems. F	Pain control P It's hard to be natural around patient. F Everyone's acting different. P/F	The minister's visits don't help. P/F
Unspoken	Mutilation distress P/F (separately) Lack of privacy P	How and what to tell relatives and friends? P/F	Guilt about not giving patient "everything" F Are finances O.K.? P	They aren't letting <u>me</u> have any say anymore. P Displaced anger F Confusion P/F John: No one seems to notice me. F Walter: I miss my "real" mom. F	If only the minister would talk about important things instead of just baseball. P

COLUMBIA-MONTOUR HOME HEALTH SERVICES, INC.
EXTENDED CARE PROGRAM (HOSPICE CONCEPT)

THE DYING PERSON'S "BILL OF RIGHTS"

I have the right to be treated as a living human being until I die.

I have the right to maintain a sense of hopefulness, however changing its focus may be.

I have the right to be cared for by those who can maintain a sense of hopefulness, however changing this might be.

I have the right to express my feelings and emotions about my approaching death in my own way.

I have the right to participate in decisions concerning my care.

I have the right to expect continuing medical and nursing attention even though "cure" goals must be changed to "comfort" goals.

I have the right not to die alone.

I have the right to be free of pain.

I have the right to have my questions answered honestly.

I have the right not to be deceived.

I have the right to have help from and for my family in accepting my death.

I have the right to die in peace and dignity.

I have the right to retain my individuality and not be judged for my decisions, which may be contrary to beliefs of others.

I have the right to discuss and enlarge my religious and/or spiritual experiences, whatever these may mean to others.

I have the right to expect that the sanctity of the human body will be respected after death.

I have the right to be cared for by caring, sensitive, knowledgeable people who will attempt to understand my needs and will be able to gain some satisfaction in helping me face my death.

The Institute for Consumer Policy Research of the Consumers Union Foundation (Mount Vernon, NY) conducted a study* of forty families that had recently experienced the loss of a family member after a lengthy illness. Experiences in hospitals, hospice inpatient settings, and home care programs were evaluated through in-depth interviews. The study indicated that family members thought that hospice units handled pain more effectively than did traditional hospitals; medication was administered regularly in a hospice setting but was administered only after pain and tension had mounted to uncomfortable levels in a hospital. Personal care was given with attention to the patient's psychological needs. Hospice care resulted in relief of depression and in self-esteem achieved by being enabled to contiinue with activities of daily living, and brought out the patient's best qualities in coming to terms with worsening illness and approaching death.

The family members believed that hospice care met their own psychological needs as well. Hospices took specific steps to strengthen family relations, facilitate communication among family members, and bring about reconciliation of real or imagined differences.

The interviews strongly suggested that hospices deal well with the problems that people associate with hospitals.

*Reported in an unpublished paper "Life Support: Families Speak About Hospital, Hospice and Home Care for the Fatally Ill" by Margaret Gold, Ph.D.

the scene. To a son or daughter who has not thought out the issues involved, the very thought of anything other than cure may, for the moment, seem appalling. Such a person who knows little about hospice may oppose the process.

2. The patient and members of the family may belong to different denominations that have differing approaches to rituals or practices for the dying. As long as the patient is conscious, her or his wishes may be honored. But if the patient appears to be unconscious, family members may want to follow practices that are contrary to those that the patient wants to observe.

3. At some time in the past the patient and spouse may have been separated or divorced. The well partner arrives on the scene with ideas that are quite different from those of the patient.

In each of these examples, considerable attention needs to be directed to possible differences of opinion regarding rights.

MEETING THE NEEDS

A logical outcome of a church's study of hospice may well be the development of an action plan based on the material in this book and the findings of the parish committee. In the development of such a plan the participation of a hospice nurse, physician, social worker, or pastoral care worker would be most helpful.

It may also be helpful during this process to return from time to time to the family needs chart shown on page 13. As the group discusses how the needs could best be met, and how the church could most appropriately assist within its purview, considerable progress will have been made.

4

QUALITY OF LIFE— WHAT DOES IT MEAN?

Everyone has a right to quality of life for as long as life lasts. No two individuals or families would probably define quality in exactly the same way, and therefore the community is an aggregation of many perceptions of quality that, when combined, form networks of community interrelationships.

If everyone has a right to quality of life, then it follows that no one has a right to define quality for someone else. This is a particularly crucial distinction in health care. It is not the responsibility of the physician, the nurse, or other health workers to make qualitative decisions for someone who happens to be ill.

Hospice care is based on the inherent right of each person (and each family) to participate in the caregiving process and determine goals, objectives, and desired outcomes insofar as physical condition permits.

QUALITY OF LIFE EXERCISE

An understanding of the importance of quality is essential for those seeking to make hospice care as effective as possible. After completing the Quality of Life grid below, church groups will be better able to comprehend the meaning of this concept.

Quality of Life Grid

	Outlook	Health	Time	Spiritual strength	Personal fulfillment
Economic					
Housing					
Family					
Possessions					
Community					
World					

The exercise may be used in successive stages. First ask individual members of the group to reply as individuals. Then the questions could be answered from the standpoint of the family of which each person is a part. Finally, each person could reply from the perspective of one dying of a terminal illness, and from the perspective of members of the family. It might be interesting to ask different groups within the church to share their conclusions. Some quality of life issues for hospice care may be defined as follows:

Time sufficient to care. Hospice care is based on the necessity for caregivers to be granted sufficient time to deal with the feelings and concerns of patient and family. Such psychosocial issues cannot be thought through—much less discussed—in a ten-minute home visit to a patient. Inpatient care provides for someone to be there to talk at different times of the day or night, although whether a caseload allows time to do so is another issue. For home care again the provision of such time is a major question of delivery of care.

Environment for care. What environment is most conducive to hospice care? Natural human instinct tends to favor the familiar surrounding of home as the ideal locale of care, but in some family situations the family members are not home a sufficient amount of time to care for one who is ill. Or the family may want to use an inpatient center for other reasons.

Expertise of caregivers. Unfortunately many health care professionals were prepared for their vocations without sufficient training in the art of openly discussing and coping with the imminence of death. It *is* difficult, to be sure, but hospice programs employ people who are usually adept in using the coping mechanisms that are necessary. And orientation and training resources are available, as noted in Resources for Study, Education, and Training.

The entire hospice philosophy and methods of care are devoted to enhancing quality of life through the ways in which hospice paid and volunteer staff members provide warm and compassionate care for all those affected by the illness.

Right to quality of life. When the early leaders of our nation declared in the Declaration of Independence the "right to life, liberty, and the pursuit of happiness," these grand phrases, which Fourth of July speeches tend to emphasize, were essentially talking about quality of life. Patient and family experience with hospice care tends to note a high degree of satisfaction with the care received. Such satisfaction is the result of the importance given to issues of quality. Indeed, everyone has a right to as much quality of life as society can make possible whether one is well or ill.

Questions of denial. It is disturbing to note from time to time statements that, owing to the high costs of health care and the increasing longevity of the age of the population, society may eventually come to the point of requiring a decision as to whether or not a given person should be allowed to continue to survive at the expense of others. Such a triage approach is incompatible with the right to quality of life. And hospice care, provided it is universally available, makes such an approach unnecessary.

ENVIRONMENT ENHANCES QUALITY OF CARE*

The recognition of the importance of the environment in whch hospice care is delivered is paramount to the assurance and maintenance of quality care for patients and their families. Because the hospice environment originates in the home, a function of the home care component of hospice is to sustain the people who constitute the patient's family in order that the continuity of that which is familiar and comfortable may add to the quality of life that hospice care seeks to make possible.

The continuity of care within the home is, in turn, possible because of the availability of inpatient care at any time in which problems arise in the provision of care at home. Hospice inpatient philosophy, therefore, looks at the basics of what makes a home a home and attempts to capture the essence of home in the inpatient setting.

From the patient's perspective, mobility is usually a past experience that the home setting encourages. The Connecticut Hospice recognizes the quality of mobility and provides space, doors wide enough to permit the

*From 1984 annual report of The Connecticut Hospice.

passage of beds, and beds functional in terms of motion in order that mobility may be brought to any immobile patient.

There is a quality of light, the openness of windows above and beside patient areas, the need for a view, and the perspective of a natural setting with nearby populations relating the setting to the community in which hospice care thrives.

There is a quality of space, especially that involving thoughtful provisions for family needs: pantries for food preparation, rooms for counseling, the Commons for community gatherings, hallways wide enough for conversation, patient/family living rooms with ample provision for sensitivity, greenhouse corridors full of light and growing plants. There is a special quality of the viewing room uniquely meant for saying good-bye. There is an inside and outside quality for the preschool with its room for laughter and growth.

The Connecticut Hospice, because of its unique combination of home care experience and inpatient design, adds dimensions of quality that deepen the meaning of patient/family care by enhancing life for as long as it lasts.

5

SPIRITUAL PAIN
AND SPIRITUAL STRENGTH

As already seen, within the hospice framework the alleviation of pain and other symptomatic help are essential if the patient and family are to achieve sufficient comfort to find a degree of quality of life.

Considerable attention has been given in hospice literature to the medical and pharmacological aspects of pain control and to the influence of psychosocial issues on the patients and families cared for by hospice programs. But little has been written about spiritual pain, which represents a source of discomfort and turmoil for many patients from a variety of religious faiths.

What is spiritual pain? According to Bess Bailey, R.N., M.S.N., Director of Support Services of The Connecticut Hospice,

> Spiritual pain is a sense of separation from or a feeling of being abandoned by one's source of inner strength, resulting in difficulty in experiencing relief from such feelings as guilt, need for forgiveness, remorse, meaninglessness, and dread of death and the unknown.*

Exactly! Spiritual pain represents a threshold many patients cross during their last journey. The hospice patient experiences this pain in the depths of his or her own soul and wants and needs a strength to correspond to every facet of the pain.

But spiritual pain can also be issue-oriented. Betsey Lewis, M.A., Connecticut Hospice Education Specialist, adds another dimension: "living with unresolved issues for which there seems no possibility of achieving a resolution." And some people view the matter from an ecclesiastical perspective; they believe that spiritual pain is a feeling of separation from God or the church.

The hospice patient will often discuss these matters with the nurse, the physician, and the social worker as well as with the chaplain. Robert P. Zanes, M.D., Vice-President for Medical Affairs of The Connecticut Hospice, says that patients sometimes call him "Father"! Each listener has a unique contribution to make, depending on personal outlook and experiences. But the patient may hope for some special insight, or possibly a sense of assurance or forgiveness, from whoever represents his or her own local church, with regard to spiritual pain.

Herein the church pastoral caregiver will note at once a blurring of roles within hospice. Spiritual issues are not the exclusive turf of the pastor any more than counseling is the property of the social worker or the psychologist.

Although at times church rites and rituals, such as the administration of communion, fulfill a most

*From conference held at The Connecticut Hospice as preparation for this book.

20

important role from the perspective of the patient and the patient's needs, helpful ministry to spiritual pain may not include any of these events. Parish caregivers, then, may discover a special kind of vitality in being part of the hospice quest for quality of life.

What are the characteristics of spiritual pain?

Certainly many things might be described as part of it, but at least ten identifiable aspects of spiritual pain are commonly experienced by dying patients and members of their families. Familiarity with these general aspects can facilitate understanding of individual patient/family situations.

The Spiritual Pain chart, which follows, was developed by the Rev. Tim Steeves of the Pastoral Care staff of The Connecticut Hospice and was subsequently added to by several colleagues during the preparation of this book.

_____

Ten Aspects of Spiritual Pain*

This chart represents a universally understood typology of ten aspects of spiritual pain that are commonly experienced by dying patients and members of their families. Pastoral caregivers within the local church may wish to add other aspects growing out of their own experiences.

Abandonment	A feeling of being forgotten by God. Jesus experienced it on the cross. "My God, my God, why hast thou forsaken me? [Matt. 27:46]."
Anger	As in Psalm 88:14: "O Lord, why dost thou cast me off? Why dost thou hide thy face from me?" Anger may be directed toward either God or people.
Betrayal	A feeling similar to abandonment, but with an extra valance. In abandonment one might feel forgotten. Betrayal goes a step further. God has turned against me; trust has been violated.
Despair	Being without hope. Having a sense that there is nowhere to turn.
Fear, dread	What does death mean? What will it bring? Where? May be

directed toward the process of dying or toward what comes afterward. "My Father, if it be possible, let this cup pass from me [Matt. 26:39]." (From the agony of Jesus in the Garden of Gethsemane.)

Guilt	Feelings of self-recrimination, of having "left undone those things which I ought to have done, and done those things which we ought not to have done."† Or the feeling that death is a punishment for misdeeds and as such, deserved.
Meaninglessness	A feeling that life is without purpose, that there is no fundamental meaning in life.
Regret	The sadness associated with irreversibility, of dreams that must remain unfulfilled, of a deeper painful wish or longing for that which cannot be.
Self-pity	Look at me, O God, poor wretch that I am. Why me? Why should I be in this condition?
Sorrow, remorse	Profound sadness. A common theme in the Bible, as when Jesus approaches the house of the ruler whose daughter has just died (Matthew 9:18). Especially apt to be associated with impending separation from those one loves.

_____

From a church perspective, for every aspect of spiritual pain there is a source of spiritual strength. It is the special mission of the pastoral caregiver to enable such sources, listed in the following table, to be marshaled by the patient.

Sources of Spiritual Strength

Forgiveness	Of others, of self, of God. It marks a turning point, the opening of new doors, in the journey through life, a kind of "spiritual relaxation."

†Adapted from "A General Confession," *The Book of Common Prayer* (New York: Oxford University Press, 1944), p. 6.

Church	The community of interrelationships that offer help in a variety of ways.
God	"God is our refuge and strength, a very present help in trouble [Ps. 46:1]." "I will lift up my eyes to the hills. From whence does my help come? [Ps. 121:1]." God represents the absolute, total, unwavering power of the ages, always present, never failing.
Hope	For today and all that it can bring; to be able to give and receive love; for two weeks of quality of life; for an immortality of impact on those one loves; for reunion with loved ones in the life beyond; for eternal life in all its glory.
Jesus Christ	The incarnation of God into human dimensions, the love of God made manifest in the flesh. "The Word became flesh and dwelt among us, full of grace and truth [John 1:14]." The perfect sacrifice of God's son for our redemption, imperfect as we are.
Prayer	A personal conversation with God; an opening of doors with implicit sharing of hopes, yearnings, and intercessions for those to be left behind. An act of worship and an act of personhood.
Presence	Just to be where one is needed, and thereby symbolize an ever-present, but sometimes unrealized, divine presence, is to demonstrate its meaning.
Rites, sacraments	Specific, familiar, comfortable, and holy ways of experiencing and re-experiencing the most meaningful aspects of one's own faith and devotion.
Silence	Not to have to say anything, and be comfortable about it, is to experience but one part of silence. To commune with reality, to absorb the fullness of the moment, to experience the discipline of waiting so that the next sound may be more personal or meaningful.
Trust	"Those who trust in the Lord are like Mount Zion, which cannot be moved, but abides for ever [Ps. 125:1]." One cannot see to the other side, or know exactly what will yet happen on this side; but wait and see with anticipation.

Both hospice and parish caregivers will want to get hold of this material in such a way as to enhance practical usage and applications in working with dying patients and their families. One method of doing this is the development of a working chart as a tool. An example of such a chart is the following, which grew out of a series of discussions within The Connecticut Hospice.

Aspects Of Spiritual Pain

This chart is a tool for understanding the aspects of the spiritual pain being experienced by a particular patient or family. Such a record is not made judgmentally, but rather to assist caring, and thus to

	1	2	3	4	5
Abandonment					
Anger					
Betrayal					
Despair					
Fear, dread					
Guilt					
Meaninglessness					
Regret					
Self-pity					
Sorrow, remorse					

help people offer support and comfort in the most appropriate ways possible. Use initials such as *P* or *O* to identify the patient, spouse, or other important persons in the picture. Place these symbols on the chart, using one for little or no evidence of spiritual pain and 5 for strong, pronounced evidence.

_____

For those who find it easier to think of people on a continuum, with individuals falling somewhere between two opposite poles on each topic, the Spiritual Worksheet below may be useful. It was adapted and developed by Vicki R. Hultine of the North Memorial Medical Center Hospice of Robbinsdale, Minnesota. (Used by permission.)

SOURCES OF SPIRITUAL STRENGTH

Assessment of the component parts of pain (spiritual or otherwise) represents only the first step. How do hospice caregivers help patients and families with spiritual pain?

Care for the spiritual needs of those in pain—and this indeed constitutes all hospice patients and members of their families to some degree—clearly begins through the offering of sources of spiritual strength. Any member of the interdisciplinary team may offer or refer to such sources in the course of individual dealings with patients and their families, and congregational representatives will certainly highlight them in the course of ministry.

The chart on pages 21–22 listing Sources of Spiritual Strength opens the door for further consideration of such personal resources. These sources will differ in accordance with religious body, the perceptions of those being served, and the framework within which one approaches caregiving in a time of dying.

_____

Spiritual Worksheet

North Memorial Medical Center Hospice
Robbinsdale, Minnesota

These observations are the subjective assessment of the caregivers. They are not for the purpose of judging a patient or a family, but rather to help them make their needs and wishes known so that the caregiving team may most appropriately assist them in healing, comforting, grieving, and celebrating life and death.

1. Indicate the patient's position on the continuum by an X, the spouse's by an O. _____ significant other, etc. Notes may be made as needed.

Awareness of the_____ holy	Out of touch with transcendent
Struggle_____	Serenity
Acceptance of_____ reality	Denial
Alienation_____	Connection/ communion
Trust_____	Defensiveness
Despair at_____ limits	Acceptance of limits
Meaning in_____ suffering	Avoidance of emotional pain
Feeling guilty_____	Feeling forgiven

2. The following questions are designed to help you explore with the patient and the family their spiritual journeys.

RELIGIOUS PRACTICE

a. How do you express your spirituality?
b. How do you feel about your spiritual expression/practice?

BELIEFS AND MEANING

a. How would you describe your philosophy of life?
b. How are you feeling about your philosophy at this time?
c. What are the word pictures of images of your life and afterlife?
d. What art, music, nature, or symbols are important to you? How might they be used at this time?
e. What are the significant and special memories of your life?
f. Do you have any last requests or wishes?

23

a. How do you understand hope?
b. For what do you hope?

3. Date: _____

_____   _____
Signature and Title   *Signature and Title*

From the perspective of the local church, there can be no doubt as to those sources that the parish's own progam of education and nurture would have fostered among its own people. These sources, therefore, represent the unique gifts that a community of Christian caring would bring to those who have entrusted themselves to their own local church.

HOW HOSPICE MINISTERS TO SPIRITUAL PAIN

Robert P. Zanes, M.D., points out that for people who are dying, spirituality is very close to the surface. Discussions with physicians and other caregivers frequently bring it to the fore.

William Shakespeare, in *Macbeth*, says, "Give sorrow words; the grief that does not speak whispers the o'er fraught heart and bids it break." Hospice care provides opportunity for verbalization of feelings. Persuading a patient to tell stories of earlier remembered days, either in person or occasionally by means of a tape recorder, is a helpful technique. In the home setting a hospice worker may ask to see photographs of happy moments of that past. "Tell me about the illness, about the death, and what it was like." "It sounds as though you are angry about something. Tell me what you think."

Hospice care emphasizes the granting of permission for the expression of anger or the expression of a feeling of guilt. Our culture is not tuned to awareness of such feelings or the need to express them.

Hospice care expresses the meaning and importance of silence. Many who visit hospice patients are afraid of saying the wrong thing. But Bess Bailey says that a good general rule is that when one is worried about saying the right thing, it is

perfectly fine to not say anything. Most spiritual pain is alleviated by one's own expression, not by the words uttered by others. Silence is a powerful tool for helping people to talk, Bailey says.

Hospice care also highlights the extreme importance of forgiveness, of people toward one another, of all of us from God. No matter how far one has strayed, says Dr. Zanes, one can always come back.

THE NURTURING ROLE OF THE LOCAL CONGREGATION

The local congregation is charged with the spiritual care of its parishioners. Recognition of factors leading to spiritual pain at the time preceding death could well encourage at least three responses:

(1) development of adult educational forums, courses, and programs; (2) the preparation of sermons designed to increase understanding of issues related to spiritual care; and (3) a constant awareness of factors leading to helpful intervention at a time of crisis.

Hospice caregivers cite the following as major parts of such an approach:

1. The congregation offers to the dying person a validation of his or her entire life as a complete entity. Such a life is not a segmented phenomenon presented for scrutiny at the times a terminal illness strikes. Any individual *is* what he or she has always been. One who sees the patient for the first time on a hospice assessment visit may be unaware that an elderly man was once a noted community leader, or that an elderly woman was once a charismatic teacher known for intellectual insights and an ability to lead the young.

The dying process is part of a lifelong continuum in which a life most often continues as it has before. Approaching death will not usually create a sudden transformation. Death will come as life came, and a patient will die as he or she has lived.

Congregations can certainly help to facilitate a whole view of life for one another long before a diagnosis of terminal illness occurs. Church rolls can be a repository of biographical experiences as well as of human and divine insights, all of which may intersect at the time hospice care becomes appropriate.

2. Congregations are especially suited never to lose sight of the tremendous importance of hope. Hope is of the very essence of Christianity. No Christian can ever lose sight of hope in its eternal dimensions. But for patients (and their families) hope may come in small doses also. Hope is being able to be present for a family event next month. Hope is knowing that for a few weeks, pain can be controlled so that one can think about unfinished business. Hope is knowing that one's family will be receiving the supportive help they need. And, yes, hope is. . .maybe, a cure.

3. By their very nature, congregations possess a kind of persuasive authority. The hospice caregiving team will want people to know that it is all right to reflect guilt, to express anger, to utter expressions of human aggravation or disturbance. But the pastoral representatives of a congregation can go a step further; they can give permission to do these things. This is possible from a religious perspective—a believer has as much right to do these things as anyone else. And it is possible from purely human perspective—one is not upsetting another by so doing.

4. Pastoral caregivers will want to be sensitive to special or unusual aspects of being ill—and of dying. The dying person, for example, may feel exactly the opposite of the way the average member of the church does about seasonal observances such as Advent, with its preparation for Christmas, or Lent, as the road to Easter. Both patients and hospice staff members may be unusually distressed during a holiday season. There is a kind of irony in preparing for joy simultaneously with preparing for death and loss. Thus it is a difficult time to be ill or to care for the dying. *And the cues for how the patient wants to be responded to must, as always, come from the patient.*

THE CHURCH MEMBER BECOME HOSPICE ALLY

Hospice care always begins with gentle assessment of patient/family needs and wants. This stripping away of preconceptions, expectations, stereotypes can facilitate the unfolding of the true spiritual position of individuals. It can enable freedom from ought-to-be's and a sharing of both yearnings and accomplishments of spirit. It can form the basis of a ministry of reconciliation.

Concretely, hospice offers a channel for restoration of spiritual wholeness. Where there has been an actual break from the church, some form of reconciliation can be implemented. But even active church members may have existed in a sort of separation from the church, a by-rote or formalized relationship. Nonjudgmental awareness of this may provide an opportunity for deepening of faith, for a final escape from barriers of indifference or assumed incompatibility. And here is a perfect role for the church member-become-hospice ally.

—Betsey Lewis, M.A.

How can a local church plunge into dying and death issues? The following illustrates what the Meriden (New Hampshire) Congregational Church has done.

LOCAL CHURCH STUDY OF DYING AND DEATH ISSUES

The Board of Deacons of a small rural church have discussed the need for an educational program that would be helpful to them in ministering to the people of their church and community. The minister of the church, in response to requests to deal with the issue of death, suggested that the deacons might become the nucleus of a group within the church that would be prepared to provide a ministry to one another in the event of the death of one of the members. This idea received considerable support among the deacons, and it was decided to pursue this idea by consulting people who were knowledgeable in the field of death and dying.

The result was the holding of a Retreat on Death and Dying, beginning on Friday and ending on Saturday evening. Ground rules for the retreat recognized that although the goal of forming a group able to minister to its members might not be reached during the retreat, each participant would benefit. The need to respect the privacy of each member of the group was recognized, as were the need to keep the program from becoming "too heavy" and the need to communicate outcomes to parents, spouses, and children.

Leaders were Doreen Schweizer of the Hospice of the Upper Valley, Lebanon, New Hampshire, and the Rev. Gregory Marshall of the Congregational Church of Meriden, New Hampshire.

The informal agenda, entitled "Really Wanting to Live: Putting Dying and Death in Its Proper Place," was as follows:

I.   DYING: PART OF OUR LIVES   *Friday evening*

    A.   Introduction—ourselves, the retreat, current theories
    B.   *Dying*—a film and discussion
    C.   Personal assessment—a work sheet to aid reflection
    D.   Evening worship celebration

II. HELPING: LESSONS FROM OUR OWN EXPERIENCE   *Saturday morning*

    A.   Morning worship celebration
    B.   Active listening—sharing our thoughts on dying
    C.   Loss and grief—sharing the experience of a loss
    D.   Identification of effective ways of helping others

III. FREE TIME   LUNCH   RECREATION

IV. DEATH: THE PRACTICAL ISSUES   *Saturday afternoon*

    A.   The significance of funeral practices
    B.   Our own funeral plans
    C.   How to help others

V.   RENEWAL   *Saturday evening*

    A.   Reflection—evaluate and share programs
    B.   Integration—communication with family and friends
    C.   Future directions—a postretreat meeting
    D.   Covenant making
    E.   Worship celebration

REV. GREGORY W. MARSHALL, MINISTER

6

THE LOCAL CHURCH AND BEREAVEMENT

Hospice programs have been challenged, as the movement has developed, to provide bereavement support for family members for up to a year after the patient's death. Specialized bereavement teams have been created, primarily consisting of volunteers trained for a unique style of grief work. Because many reimbursement mechanisms do not pay for care after the patient's death, there has been every encouragement to maintain the volunteer nature of such work, albeit with the addition of professional leaders who can impart their skills to the volunteers and develop methods to assure the validity of the care given.

Highly skilled bereavement workers are quick to identify the dangers involved in placing inexperienced helpers in situations where they could easily be confronted with psychiatric and psychological problems that are beyond their competence to manage. It is hoped that churches, as they view hospice from the outside, can find local, highly skilled people who are comfortable in encouraging others to express the deep pain that they feel, and can do so without being judgmental or seeking to impose their own agendas.

The role of a professional social worker, psychologist, or other person who is comfortable in the presence of pain, who understands the grief process, and who can provide leadership to bereavement workers is essential. In some areas such a person might be identified on a regional basis and work with several hospice programs in the area.

Every hospice bereavement program has been faced with the necessity of refusing participation to well-meaning people who are basically seeking to work out their own problems. Most of us begin our approach to caregiving with what Linda Chase, M.S.W., Bereavement Coordinator for The Connecticut Hospice, calls "rescue fantasies" for those who are suffering. Many of us, she believes, are first motivated to be helpers by such fantasies. "It is by acknowledging that we have them that we can step back and understand what our role is to be," she says. But if rescue fantasies cloud our judgments, it would be all too easy, she points out, for a person who has decided that the best way to handle personal grief is to put it aside and get on with living to tell someone else to "do what I am doing and stop being so upset."

Hospice bereavement work is based on certain principles that are mandatory if such care is to fulfill its objectives. One such principle is that people need to grieve, each in his or her own way; indeed, some of the necessary training is to enable bereavement workers to stand by while a bereaved person moves through successive stages of grief. Another principle is that the introduction of a new person into the family equation after the patient's death provides rich, new resources for family members to bring to the surface feelings and issues that must be worked through before they can go on to other things. Yet another is that it is not the role of a team member to provide support for a family member; rather, as Linda Chase says, the role is to help the grieving get their own supports going. She adds that being comfortable with disengaging a relationship with a bereaved family is essential; some people enjoy having others depend on them. The task in hospice bereavement work is to prepare the family being helped for termination.

Bereavement work requires *total* confidentiality on the part of the worker. Such confidentiality works against having a worker who has already developed a friendship with the person through the church, the neighborhood, or other organizations. It could well be said that in a rural or town/village setting, regional networking would be advisable so that no bereavement workers would work with residents of their own town.

All hospice care, including bereavement, requires the ability to let those being served set the agenda. It would be all too easy for someone in a religious setting, during the bereavement intervention, to inject her or his own biblical or theological understandings into the equation. To do so, however, would be inappropriate.

Those selected for bereavement work—and there clearly needs to be a selection process—need to possess a high degree of self-awareness and be able to help others feel confident because they feel confident themselves. They must respect the styles and beliefs of others, although these may be radically different from their own. Linda Chase and the Connecticut Hospice Bereavement Team think that a year and a half should have elapsed since a potential team member suffered a personal bereavement.

What is the relationship of the local church to such a bereavement effort? Clearly the parish will be an obvious source for those who want to dedicate themselves to bereavement work on a community level. During the time that the community hospice team is serving a parish member during a grief experience, the church will want to be supportive in as many ways as possible (see chapter 7). And as the family member approaches the time for termination of the hospice contacts, the church will be ready to provide channels for carrying out the next stages of the person's life.

There may well be parishes in which the local community of faith decides to try to provide bereavement support for its own parishioners, thus serving not only families that have experienced a terminal illness, but also those who have faced other catastrophes, such as a death resulting from an automobile accident, a fire, or a heart attack. The hospice experience indicates the strong need to develop such a ministry on a highly skilled and professional basis.

There is need, in such a setting, to differentiate between being helpful and supportive in practical ways—as might normally be expected as members of an extended family help one another through difficult times—and the provision or application of skilled bereavement intervention. An analogy would be that there may be times when a church member should be referred for counseling by a mental health professional. Such a referral would be a confidential matter. But some of the other church members might sense that there was a special problem and offer their own continuing friendship. When a death occurs in the parish, people will always want to help, but that help should not be confused with bereavement grief work.

Lucile Hutchinson, who has served as a member of the Connecticut Hospice bereavement team for many years, accents the tremendous importance of providing support for those who are involved in bereavement activity (as well as other phases of hospice care). The bereavement team itself needs support. A pastor who is involved in intensive grief work with parishioners needs support. Where will this support come from?

Within the team itself, whoever has been designated to provide professional leadership supports the other team members. Expressing appreciation for what the team does is obvious yet essential. Considerable time will be spent discovering how best to support the bereavement professional as well as other hospice interdisciplinary workers. And on a community or regional level those who do not have such channels will need to develop their own support mechanisms.

Those who are involved in bereavement care must receive sufficient training, both initially and on an in-service basis. See Selected Annotated Bibliography on Dying and Death and Resources for Study, Education, and Training for additional resources and suggestions.

7

STRATEGIES FOR COPING WITH LOSS

Bess Bailey, R.N., M.S.N.*

LOSS AS LIFE EXPERIENCE

Members of a bereavement support group at The Connecticut Hospice were asked what they would say about the experiences of loss and strategies to cope with it. One of the strongest responses was from a widower who said: *"Time* doesn't heal grief; *grievers* heal grief. It's hard work, and a little help goes a long way."

All of us are experts on loss, in that we have repeatedly experienced the painful task of letting go of someone or something we were not ready or willing to be without.

DEVELOPMENTAL LOSSES

When asked at what age they had their first experience with loss, people usually answer "5," "10," "13," "23," perhaps thinking back to a first death in the family. Actually our own birth is our first experience with loss. We were thrust—not by our own choice—out of the warm, moist world of the womb into the dry, cool air of disconnectedness. In the first moments of life a newborn's face

reflects confusion, fear, rage, pain, and anguish. Although *we* know the wonders that lie ahead for the child, the infant is, at first, not happy with the drastic change from womb to world.

Very early in life we must *let go* of one way of operating in order to move ahead to a more advanced way, giving up the breast and mastering self-feeding, progressing from crawling to walking, gaining enough bladder control to stop wearing diapers and become toilet trained. But we often do so with reluctance, substituting thumb for breast in order not to lose the entire experience all at once.

As young students of loss we exercise the reality of coming and going by practicing. We have seen children sit in a playpen and drop toys out onto the floor. We put them back in the playpen and notice the delight with which the baby lets go again, hoping that we will keep up our part of choreographed dance by returning the toy. The game of peekaboo is Loss 201 in early schooling. Peekaboo gives the baby a sense of *control* over the experience of having someone disappear and then return. Later in life the need and wish to control the going and returning is still with us. Although our intellect tells us that we don't have that power, we will seek it.

One day that all parents remember is the first day the school bus picks up their kindergartners. With mixed feelings one dressed one's cherished

*Director of Support Services, Connecticut Hospice. The author acknowledges the significant contributions of Peter Lynch, M.S.W., A.C.S.W., to the ideas expressed in this chapter.

former pre-schooler in a first real school outfit, and with a lump in the throat one saw the huge yellow bus round the corner and open its doors to take on board one's baby! Of course one is proud. One wants a child to go to school, but with wistfulness one becomes aware that an era is gone forever. Many of us hide our tears behind our camera shutters. How well I recall the faces of my son and, later, daughter as they looked out the school bus window, reflecting the mixture of excitement and sadness I felt.

By the time children climb on the school bus, at the age of five or six, they have experienced an array of loss experiences, having let go of stages in their lives that will never return. They have experienced the seasons: they know that flowers and leaves die in autumn, that after winter is here for a time, spring returns. They know one season cannot come until the previous one has gone. They know that in order to sleep in a big bed, they have to give up the crib. They may know that if they want a brother or sister, they have to give up the place of being the only child to their parents. They know that if they want to learn to swim, they have to leave the baby pool and cross the "great divide" to the big people's pool.

Possibly all of this they know without ever experiencing what we would consider a loss experience, that is, the death of a loved person or a catastrophic event, such as a divorce or moving.

It is not hard to think of other developmental losses. Each birthday represents a year gained . . . and a year lost. I clearly remember my sixth birthday when I wistfully realized that I would never be five again. There is tremendous stress on birthdays, when one feels that one should be at one's best; there is ambivalence involved as one moves forward into a new identity and a new age.

Pets are an extremely valuable experience in loss for families, and I encourage families at least to invest in goldfish when children are growing up. It is a good experience to have something to tend, nourish, care about, and then lose because it has died. The loss of a pet should never be minimized.

Experiences that children have during the summer, such as going to camp or otherwise being away from home and having that incredible—and inevitable—homesickness, also illustrate the deepening development of loss experiences. Working through such experiences, realizing that they subside with time, and relinquishing the experience of the summer as a whole is an intense time. These are opportunities for adults to teach children about change, new experiences, and the sadness, as well as the reward, that accompanies letting go and moving on.

Certainly the transition to puberty involves many conflicting feelings, on the part of both the children and their parents. The changes that accompany puberty are positive, but they also are a sign that the innocence of childhood is gone. Never underestimate the early dating and love experiences that children have. Parents often minimize such experiences; rather, they should acknowledge them and encourage their children to find ways of expressing the pain they feel.

Getting married or deciding to make a commitment to another person or to a religious order is, in fact, a loss experience because that kind of commitment means letting go of other options. The tears shed on our wedding day may be partly for the single life we leave behind. They can also come from the letting go of the ideal mate for a real one.

Having children is a developmental loss experience—happy though it may be—because it also brings a change that, by definition, includes loss. We have to let go of the way things were before the new person arrived. Moving from one town to another, or even from house to house, is a loss experience that may assume crisis proportions. Letting go of all the support people, groups, services, and mechanisms that we depend on is a difficult thing to do.

Another developmental loss we experience as we grow older is the way our bodies change. Up through early adulthood they are usually changing for the better, but as we age we begin to deteriorate. For some people letting go of the old body image and embracing a current phase of life bring a grieving response. Also, as we grow older we let go of our dreams about what our lives will be like. Options change, and letting go of an idea of life as including those options is hard for some people to manage.

In later years loss becomes a prevalent and almost daily experience. One's health can deteriorate in many small and big ways; the way one functions in society changes; one's income usually decreases. Friends get sick, change their life-style, or die. Much work on loss of this kind needs to be done in retirement communities, where loss is a frequent life experience.

So, although it may sound like a cliché, we are born to lose; we experience loss repreatedly and constantly throughout our life journey. Most of the events are normal, usual, developmental life experiences. These repeated growth experiences are helping us to prepare for bigger, deeper losses. They are practice sessions, rehearsals, for the unexpected and less acceptable losses.

UNWELCOME LOSSES

Death is an unwelcome loss and one of the severest, although others can be just as unacceptable, including loss of health to chronic illness and disabilities, loss of body parts, loss of spouse—and even children—through divorce, loss of income and identity through job changes or retirement, changes of relationship in families. These jarring, cataclysmic events call forth from us the more intense but nevertheless familiar feeling and behavioral response we call *grief.*

To put these unwelcome losses in the context of loss as a life experience is to emphasize one of the central truths about loss, grief, and bereavement—that without these experiences, these pains, we do not grow in life. Inherent in the sadness of loss are the incredible potential for emotional gain and a renewed contract with life itself. So even though loss is perceived as a negative word, it holds out to us the opportunity for growth, for new or renewed strength, new opportunities, insights, even wisdom.

These words will make no sense if one is currently in the midst of a significant loss experience. Although the potential for growth is great as a result of successful grieving, when one is in the process one does not feel this at all. So one needs to be gentle with oneself if one is grieving and not expect to experience gain or positive response to discussion of grief.

I am not trying to gloss over the devastating impact of major losses and subsequent bereavement on survivors. The anguish of those left behind has always concerned society and is reflected in every culture's mourning rituals.

Behavioral scientists, educators, health care professionals, and clergy are becoming increasingly concerned with describing the nature of grief and the toll it takes on survivors. A number of theories have been proposed in this regard, beginning with Sigmund Freud in 1915, who first differentiated so-called normal grief from melancholia, a pathological depression.* Subsequently Eric Lindemann, in 1944, did the first empirical study of the behavior of recently bereaved people, who had all experienced sudden death of a family member in a nightclub fire in Boston. Lindemann described the normal acute grief syndrome and coined the term grief work to refer to the griever's mental activity necessary to work toward healing of the loss.†

Shapers of public policy are also becoming aware of the toll that bereavement can take. Current interest in stress-related illness and preventive medicine is increasingly evident in allocation of grants and research funding. In 1984 a substantial report was issued by the National Institute of Mental Health, Office of Prevention, on bereavement. This comprehensive report speaks to the health consequences of bereavement and suggests preventive interventions for bereaved people as well as future research directions.‡

Although most of the work summarized here has emphasized the bereavement after the loss through death of a significant other, it is becoming increasingly clear that the reactions and needed grief work are applicable in various degrees to any major loss event.

THE JOURNEY OF GRIEF

What is this grief work that constitutes bereavement? What must we experience and do in order to cope with a loss event in our lives?

A variety of models of the grieving process have been proposed. The overview I have developed is heavily based on the work of several theorists, especially John Bowlby§ and Colin Murray Parkes.‖

"The Journey of Grief" on p. 33 shows the stages, not of an event, but of a process. It is not a description of something that is in a fixed state or that happens at a point in time. Rather, it is something that unfolds, something that is dynamic. I call this process a journey because it has a destination. In fact, it has several destinations, or goals.

*Sigmund Freud, *Mourning and Melancholia* (1917; London: Hogarth Press, 1957), vol. 14.

†Eric Lindemann, "Symptomatology and Management of Acute Grief," *American Journal of Psychiatry* 101:141–49, 1944.

‡M. Osterweis, *Bereavement: Reactions, Consequences, and Care* (Washington, DC: National Academy Press, 1984).

§J. Bowlby, "Process of Mourning," *International Journal of Psychoanalysis* 42:317–40, 1961.

‖See C.M. Parkes, *Bereavement: Studies of Grief in Adult Life* (New York: International Universities Press, 1972).

The Journey of Grief

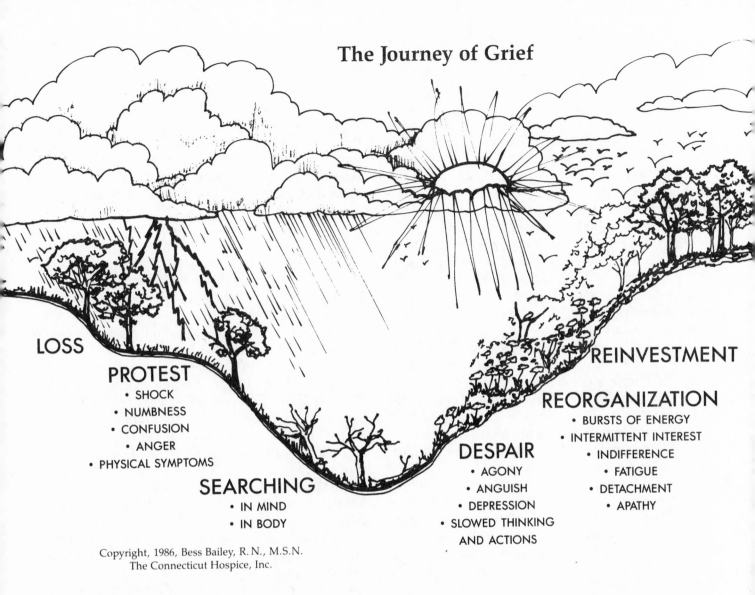

LOSS

PROTEST
- SHOCK
- NUMBNESS
- CONFUSION
- ANGER
- PHYSICAL SYMPTOMS

SEARCHING
- IN MIND
- IN BODY

DESPAIR
- AGONY
- ANGUISH
- DEPRESSION
- SLOWED THINKING AND ACTIONS

REINVESTMENT

REORGANIZATION
- BURSTS OF ENERGY
- INTERMITTENT INTEREST
- INDIFFERENCE
- FATIGUE
- DETACHMENT
- APATHY

Copyright, 1986, Bess Bailey, R.N., M.S.N.
The Connecticut Hospice, Inc.

The first goal, although it sounds easy to accomplish, is in fact difficult to achieve: acceptance of the reality of the loss. The second goal is to experience the pain of the grief. The third is to withdraw emotional energy from that which is lost, be it person, place, time of life, or state of health, and reinvest it in one's current life as it is.

Although the journey outlined here is described in terms of stages, one must always be aware that it is not a lock-step process. One moves back and forth among the stages, sometimes at intervals of days or hours, so that even in a day's time one can be in several places on the journey. In the midst of it it is hard to see a pattern, but when one pulls away and looks at the process from a distance, one can plot what is outlined here.

At one time I diagrammed the process in terms of a line that moves up and down—it looked like a graph. In a bereavement support group a young man whose mother had died decided that the outline needed more "scenery." Therefore, the diagram of the "Journey of Grief" compares the stages of feelings with the changing of the seasons, the *loss* itself beginning as an enormous electrical storm, coinciding with autumn, when everything begins to change.

After the loss the first phase or stage of the experience is *protest*. The intensity of this stage and the way it is experienced have much to do with whether there was warning of the loss, with time for anticipation, or whether the loss was sudden and unexpected. If it was sudden, the stage of protest is usually more intense and perhaps longer-lived. But even when there is an opportunity to anticipate the loss, as with a chronic illness or a troubled marriage, at the time of the actual death or leaving a combination of protest reactions takes place. The body is saying, "No! I don't like it, and I don't want it." One experiences a sense of unreality, shock, numbness. Nothing seems real or normal, including one's own self. It is a time of confusion and absent-mindedness. Some people describe a sort of hazy grayness over their visual field. It is common to lose things. Others have described getting lost in their own houses or in other familiar places. There is difficulty in organizing one's time or deciding what to do next. Anxiety begins to penetrate, and physical symptoms appear; it can be a time of great physical discomfort, manifested as tightness in the chest or throat, dryness in the mouth, and a hollowness in the stomach. The body is mobilizing itself as if for an emergency. Sleep and appetite disturbances are prevalent. Sometimes there is an overwhelming heaviness in the chest, almost as if the person had been hit by a heavy object.

Usually this sensation is relatively short-lived, lasting for hours or days, sometimes weeks. Most people do not experience strong emotions during this time, with the exception of anger. It is useful to tell people that being angry is a normal part of grieving and to help family members be especially forgiving to one another. When the anger is directed at oneself, it is experienced as guilt.

The numbness and unreality, which are merciful at the beginning, gradually begin to wear off. More and more there is a preoccupation with that which is lost. Parkes calls this period a time of *searching*. Because every layer of our psyche refuses to accept the harsh reality all at once, part of our subconscious mind thinks that the lost may still be found. Sometimes there is frustration and anger when one's attention is directed away from the loss into activities of daily living. One is drawn into doing things that might give a sense of how life used to feel, with the lost person still present.

For example, there is often a strong sense of having been visited by the person who has died. One might see that face coming toward one in a crowd, only to suddenly remember that it can't possibly be the person who has so recently died. Or one is drawn to visit places where one has felt particularly close to the person who is now dead. Or one might feel the need to do something that one formerly did with the other person or that that person did alone. Or there may be vivid dreams that include the lost person. Familiar smells of perfume or aftershave worn by the dead person seem to permeate the air. Often the searching behavior temporarily brings consolation or relief from lone-liness, but the relief fades with repeated reminders that the search is in vain.

Anger—at almost anything—can be a continuing factor during this phase. This is understandable; something has been taken from us that we do not want to be without. But often we cannot identify the anger, or we try to suppress it, only to find it bursting forth in unexpected ways at people we do not want to hurt. Again, if the anger is turned toward oneself, the guilt can be very uncomfortable.

More and more, as searching fails to bring relief from the loss, one descends into the most difficult part of the journey, the phase of *despair*. This is the part we want to avoid most. The leaves are off the trees; the weather is cold; the atmosphere is bleak. And people describe the emotions that come over them as waves of anguish. Awareness of the reality of the loss, and the pain that comes with it, wash over one with almost unbearable intensity.

It is important to note the intermittent nature of such despair. One way in which we differentiate between a normal grief journey and one that results in clinical depression is that the normal process is intermittent, whereas that of depression is more constant in its hopelessness. In grief it is natural to experience tremendous anguish, followed by times of relief from the pain. One is, basically, in a depressed state, however. It is difficult to find energy, to be interested in anything. One's thinking and actions are slowed. If a person can cry during this time, this often relieves the sadness, or at least the intensity of the feelings. Again, a good way to identify the atypical grief is to note when crying does not bring much relief.

Usually a person in the midst of such despair is able to receive warmth and caring from another person. It is a good time for those who want to be helpful to reach out and provide or offer warmth and support. It is important to know that this period of despair is longer-lived than our culture wants to believe; four to fourteen months after the death would be within a normal range. Society generally expects one to be back to normal witin six months. And we now know that this is when the difficult period of grieving is just beginning. People can be helpful to those who are going through the process by understanding the length of time this requires.

Many people try to build a bridge over the valley, going from the searching phase to the *reorganization* phase, when they find themselves sinking into the valley. Some are so frightened at the intensity of the experience that they back up and try to put a ladder across the valley of despair. Not allowing oneself to feel despair does not cause those difficult emotions to dissipate; rather, they are put away or aside, only to surface later with more complexity and difficulty of expression. The only way through the valley is to go down into it, to express and feel the sadness. After descending into the valley of despair one will find the energy to climb out again.

Then one morning one may wake up and notice how beautiful the sun looks shining through the window. The capacity to appreciate has been missing for some time. It is like the first crocus to come up in the spring. The bereaved person is again able to enjoy, to be hopeful, to be tentatively interested in life, to experience its goodness.

Such moments begin to occur more and more frequently. It is diagramed as an upward climb, for in fact it is hard work. One has to get a toehold and pull oneself up, responding to those moments of interest with action. This is the period when the divorced mother might read a book about single parenthood, or when a widow might find the energy to go to a widowed group. During this phase one may experience bursts of energy and then fall back into despair. But one's capacity to be interested in things steadily increases. If one exerts the energy, takes such toeholds and pulls oneself out of the valley, at first tentatively and then more and more strongly, one begins to invest in life as it is now.

The last phase of the journey is *reinvestment*, which involves a willingness to commit oneself to one's current relationships, to one's work and interests, and to one's new identity.

A few additional points should be made about the journey. The diagram does not really show how winding the journey is. It is cyclical in part, in that as one passes through these phases there are times when one goes backward, not forward. But each time one reverts to a previous stage, the time spent at that stage seems to be briefer; one can move out of it more quickly.

The goal of grieving is not to get over the loss. Sometimes people become stuck on the journey because they fear that they *will* get over the loss, and therefore be left as if the person who was lost was never in their lives. Rather, a healthy grieving process is one in which positive strengths are gained from the lost relationship and are incorporated into a new current life.

It is also important to be prepared for the fact that certain days, such as important personal anniversaries, and cultural holidays, such as Thanksgiving and Christmas, tend to be difficult. The anniversary phenomenon can send one way back, even to the stage of protest. Anticipating and planning for anniversary days can be helpful.

How long does the journey take? The time is quite variable. For normal grief, responding to a significant loss, we think in terms of one to three years. Our culture is not basically aware of such a timetable.

HOW TO HELP PEOPLE COPE WITH LOSS

Does everyone reach the destination? Most, but not all, can. Some people get bogged down in one phase and are not able to move on to eventual reinvestment and healing. Usually this is caused by anxiety about experiencing the pain and anguish of relinquishing the lost person or object. Grief can be atypical in its intensity and its timing.

Statistics reveal a higher morbidity and mortality rate for those who are bereaved, especially spouses, in the first two years after a death. For these people the physical symptoms of grief, combined with their state of health, are overwhelming. Stresses experienced in a marriage after the death of a child can result in a higher divorce rate for bereaved couples. Anger about the loss of a loved one or the loss of one's own health and body state can become so strong that it interferes with grief work.

Behavioral science literature is full of examples of psychological and physical problems that can surface years after a loss as a result of unresolved grief. Such people go on with their own lives but are blocked in areas of potential growth and development.

DETERMINANTS OF THE OUTCOME

What, then, determines the outcome of the grief journey? According to Parkes,* many factors influence it, including the following:

*Ibid.

1. The importance of the loss, who the person was, and the roles played by the lost person as well as the survivors. In the case of loss of health, how crucial the body image was may be most significant.
2. The age at which the loss occurs
3. The nature of the attachment to the lost person, especially the degree of ambivalence and dependency
4. Childhood experiences and how losses were handled then
5. How the loss occurred. Was it preventable, or accidental? Was it sudden, or was there warning?
6. Personality variables, especially those dealing with expression of feelings and tolerance for pain and anxiety
7. Social, cultural, religious variables
8. Secondary losses or stresses going on simultaneously: concurrent bereavements, unresolved bereavements, children at home to care for, illness of the survivor, and financial pressures
9. Social support or isolation; any close relationship helps; options available to the survivor

Thorough assessment of these variables can help identify those people who might be at risk of not entering into a healthy grieving process, and alerting involved caregivers to follow some survivors more closely than others. At our hospice and many others it has been found that about 30 percent of survivors are identified to be at higher risk and potentially in need of more help. Only 5 percent of all the families are referred to outside resources for professional long-term counseling.

Can we really help people cope with loss? Yes we can. *And* no, we cannot do it for them.

Research is new in areas of evaluating and demonstrating the effect that help has had on the outcome of grief. Some studies conducted in the past few years have shown promise that supportive help—especially in areas of encouraging expression of grief—does result in better outcomes. More research needs to be done in this area. But speaking from experience, I would offer the following observations.

The grief journey is similar in several ways to the inflammatory response, a compensatory mechanism the body uses to respond to physical injury. Both the grief journey and the inflammatory response are reactions to injury. Inflammation causes redness, pain, and swelling; grief causes injury to the spirit—yearning, pining, crying, and despair.

The potential for both responses is inherent in us, given at birth, for we are all capable of such responses. Both cause pain. Both are occasions for healing; inflammation mobilizes the healing mechanisms of blood and tissue; grief mobilizes those mechanisms that heal the spirit.

Both can go awry—inflammation, with chronic debilitation that is unresolved; grief, becoming atypical with no relief.

A wound heals from the inside out; grief does the same. If healing does not happen from the inside out, that part of the body this is injured is weakened for the next injury or occasion when it is needed. Similarly with grief; if one tries to circumvent the process and avoid the pain, one will not be able to fully reinvest oneself, and some energy will always need to be expended to keep the grief at bay.

So how does one help? In the case of inflammation the affected part is immobilized; the wound is cleaned, antibiotics are given, and rest is provided. In the case of bereavement one can support the process, encourage expression of the journey, hear the pain, recognize and support the searching, point out the landmarks in the journey, and educate about the process, and grievers can be brought together for expression and sharing.

This is not easy to do, this helping. The story of the garden of Gethsemane shows this. The disciples went to sleep during the agony. It is painful to stand by and not be able to change reality.

For people who are coping with loss, help can come from health professionals through counseling and support; from bereavement intervention self-help programs; from caring friends; from ministers, teachers, and educators; from funeral directors; from law enforcement officers (often the first on the scene); and from emergency medical personnel.

Wherever we encounter such people they are at some point on this arduous journey. We cannot walk their steps for them, but we can fall in stride next to them and be willing to listen to them tell about the trials of the journey, and perhaps even absorb some of the anger and frustration.

Blessed are those who mourn, for they shall be comforted.

—Matthew 5:4

8

HOSPICE AND AIDS*

Mary Ellen Haines and William Stackhouse†

Wherever people with AIDS (acquired immune deficiency syndrome) live, their plight presents challenges to local hospice programs that have sought to be inclusive in their service to the dying and their families. As the "Dying Person's 'Bill of Rights'" on page 15 states, "I have the right to expect continuing medical and nursing attention even though 'cure' goals must be changed to 'comfort' goals."

The local church can fulfill its own mission and at the same time strengthen service to those who are dispossessed and unwanted by learning about the AIDS situation in its area and determining how hospice is being or could be of help in meeting the needs of people with AIDS (PWAs), their families, and friends.

It is particularly difficult for a society that has grown to expect medical science to cure disease to admit that there is a new disease among us and that a cure is years away. However, in the midst of this tragic reality, it is vital that Americans affirm that AIDS is preventable and will one day be curable. With the strength of that affirmation and the empowerment of a vision of wholeness, people of faith can become a major force in the mobilization of the community to both minister to PWAs, their

families, and friends and to end this tragic pandemic. Pastoral caregivers and health care and hospice workers who willingly meet the needs of PWAs serve as public models of rational and compassionate behavior in communities that may otherwise be engulfed in fear.

It is important for church members and the citizenry as a whole to know the history of the disease and to understand projections based on the current statistics. What began in the early 1980s with the puzzling and relatively isolated deaths of individuals in high-risk categories has rapidly grown to the point of a threatening global pandemic. The World Health Organization survey in 1986 has shown seventy-four countries reporting cases of AIDS in the Americas, Europe, Africa, Asia, and Oceania and has described the spread of AIDS as a "health disaster of pandemic proportions."

Today the number of people in the United States diagnosed as having AIDS is more than 40,000; of these more than half have died. Until a cure is discovered all those diagnosed with AIDS are expected to die of its effects. In addition, the number of people in the United States estimated to be infected with the virus is 1.5 to 2 million. All of these people are assumed to be capable of spreading the virus. By 1991 it is estimated as many as 200,000 persons in the United States may have died from AIDS, 25 to 30 percent of them in that year alone. Hospice programs must prepare now to meet the challenge that caring for PWAs poses.

*Adapted from "The Pronouncement: Health and Wholeness in the Midst of a Pandemic," adopted by the United Church of Christ General Synod XVI, June 1987.

†Consultants, AIDS ministry, United Church Board for Homeland Ministries.

AIDS is an infectious disease that is caused by a retrovirus. The virus lodges in the special white blood cells (T lymphocytes) that play an important role in our immune systems, which protect us against most diseases. Most people who become infected with human immunodeficiency virus (HIV) have no immediate symptoms. An infected person may not show symptoms of disease for five to seven years. Not all infected people have progressed to disease. For some a severer form of infection occurs that is called AIDS-related complex (ARC). This form includes such symptoms as swollen lymph glands, diarrhea, night sweats, weight loss, and fatigue. AIDS is the end stage of HIV infection that results in a person having a life-threatening infection or cancer. Opportunistic infections are caused by microorganisms that take advantage of the opportunity offered by lower immunity but would seldom cause disease in people with normal biological immunity. These infections, including *Pneumocystis carinii* pneumonia, toxoplasmosis, tuberculosis, viral infections owing to herpes complex, and meningitis, are the most common causes of death in PWAs. Probably because of the weakened immune system in AIDS patients, such infections are characterized by an aggressive clinical course, resistance to therapy, a high rate of relapse, and a high incidence of drug toxicity. Kaposi's sarcoma, a cancer-producing lesion of the skin, was one of the earliest recognized manifestation of AIDS. It is believed that the incidence of the disease as a result of HIV infection is decreasing. There is now increased frequency of non-Hodgkin's lymphomas, occurring in the central nervous system, the rectum, and gastrointestinal sites, in patients with HIV antibodies. Most AIDS patients also have some clinical manifestation of neurological disease, dementia being the severest and most disabling. HIV infection progresses differently in children than in adults. Certain symptoms and illnesses are more common in children. For example, central nervous system abnormalities have been reported in 50 to 80 percent of infected children.

In the past six years the majority of diagnosed cases in the United States have been men who have had unprotected sexual contact with men; intravenous drug abusers, both men and women, who have shared dirty needles and syringes with infected others; and the sexual partners of both groups. HIV, the AIDS virus, is transmitted through infected blood or sexual secretions. Anti-body to the HIV virus has been found in saliva and tears. However, the virus concentration is much lower in these fluids than in blood or sexual secretions. No cases of HIV infection through tears or saliva have been reported. The behaviors that involve the highest risk are sharing needles and syringes and unprotected sexual contact. These modes of transmission apply to children as well as to adults. An infected woman may transmit the virus prenatally or at birth. Barriers to transmission, such as using gloves if there is to be contact with body fluids and using condoms in sexual acts, have proved effective. The risk of HIV infection through blood transfusion is currently very small in America. Caring for PWAs poses almost no threat of infection when the guidelines of the Centers for Disease Control (CDC) are followed. Many health care workers are considered at increased risk for infections such as hepatitis B because of occupational exposure to infected blood primarily through needlestick exposure or abrasion of the skin. The CDC recently conducted a study of health care workers who had reported parenteral or membrane exposure to blood or other body fluids from AIDS patients. Of these workers 4 percent developed HIV antibodies. In a comparable study of workers exposed to hepatitis B, 26 percent developed infection. The 4 percent is similar to the proportions of the U.S. population employed in health care. The church can reassure those who care for PWAs by sharing this information.

Anyone can be infected with AIDS. Blacks and Latinos are currently infected in disproportionately high numbers in every risk category, except for hemophilia-coagulation disorder. The CDC anticipate that in the future, most people will contract the virus through heterosexual contact. Black women are thirteen times more likely to get AIDS than are white women. The number of cases of AIDS in children is expected to rise. In many families with AIDS more than one child may be infected.

A ministry of health and wholeness in the midst of this potentially destructive disease involves being a life-giving presence to PWAs, their families, and caregivers. Persons with AIDS need to know that they will have life in the midst of their dying. Life-giving ministry involves adequate medical care that is both affordable and respectful of patient's rights, medical privacy, and confidentiality. Life-giving ministry involves the assurance of a home and support facilities that enable the PWA to be in a caring home except when he or she needs the special facilities that a hospital, extended-care facility, or hospice can provide. Foster care is a critical and growing need for children with AIDS who can no longer be cared for by parents who have the disease. Hospice care in the future will increasingly involve families in which one or both parents may have AIDS as well as one or more children concurrently. In such situations any opportunity for quality home care is severely hindered, if not devastated; thus there will be increasing need for family hospice care.

Life-giving ministry involves pastoral care that includes nonjudgmental listening, exploring questions of faith, prayer, reading of scripture, sharing a meal, and simply being present without any demands. Pastoral caregivers need to examine their motives, presuppositions, and limitations in offering spiritual care to PWAs. Because society has judged the current primary forms of transmission of HIV infection—sexual activity outside of a monogamous heterosexual marriage and illicit intravenous drug use—as taboo, pastoral caregivers too often communicate society's judgment, demonstrate self-righteousness, and require confession of past sins as a prerequisite of sharing God's love. In contrast, a PWA needs the presence and witness of God's unconditional love embodied in pastoral caregivers. Judgments should be put aside as a caregiver enters into and participates with a PWA in his or her experience of living with hopes, fears, problems, and joys. Some PWAs carry a sense of having done something wrong and that the disease is just punishment. Such burdens of guilt or social stigma can extend to the internal and external ex-

perience of loved ones and family members. The acceptance and supportive involvement of loved ones is an integral part of the pastoral caregiving process. When geographical distance must be crossed, or when emotional chasms between family members need to be bridged, the understanding of people of faith in a caregiving role can be redemptive.

Public advocacy for provision for and access to adequate quality services for PWAs should, by necessity, be considered an important pastoral care role. Because of fear and prejudice a community's response can be to "bury them before they are dead." The number of cases in the gay, Latino, and black communities has provided an additional opportunity to fan the flames of prejudice. The church must counter this prejudice, which has already been a serious barrier to an effective response to the pandemic. The church and society are called to confront the racial, ethnic, and sexual prejudices that have too often immobilized them.

The overall approach and philosophy of hospice care are uniquely suited and increasingly necessary to PWAs, their families, and friends. Throughout the nation PWAs have faced their disease, and society can benefit from their inspiring courage. Hospice has proved to be an increasingly significant component of care to PWAs. The Shanti Project in San Francisco has brought its hospice message and training to caregivers across the land. The hospice program at St. Vincent's Hospital in New York City has been inspirational to people throughout the East. With the help of hospice programs, PWAs will live out their lives more fully.

9

HOSPICE AND CHILDREN

Most hospice care in the United States is provided for adults. Only 22 percent of the hospices in the nation, as of 1984, care for or are willing to care for children. And the number of children served is very small.

Children's Hospice International, a unique organization established to act as an advocate and clearinghouse for hospice care for children, invited Barbara A. McCann, Director of the Accreditation Program for Hospice Care of the Joint Commission on Accreditation of Hospitals, to survey hospices in order to determine what is being done for children. Five hundred fifteen hospices responded to her survey (34 percent of those addressed).

The survey indicated that many of the hospices that do serve children fail to provide a continuum of services in both home care and inpatient settings. This was especially true of community-based hospice programs that are not affiliated with a hospital, nursing home, or other institution.

The majority of hospice programs that do service children were located, according to the survey, in areas with a population of less than 500,000 persons, and 41 percent of them were in areas of 100,000 or less. This is an interesting statistic, inasmuch as most large pediatric hospitals and university-related research centers are located in urban areas.

The average length of stay for children was less than that for adults in the same programs. The study indicated that children tend to be referred at the very end of the illness, before death.

Hospices that serve children tend to lack all the prerequisite interdisciplinary team services; 75 percent provide only social work, spiritual, and bereavement services.

The survey noted lack of adequate reimbursement for care for children; in fact some of the hospice programs did not charge for such services.

It is clear that much attention needs to be directed toward determining what kind of care is needed for children. This matter needs to be analyzed in concert with the professional pediatric community. If the local parish contains children who are in need of hospice care, an appropriate part of the study of hospice could well be an analysis of who serves children and where.

Children's Hospice International, the only national organization dedicated to hospice care of children, describes itself as follows:

PEDIATRIC HOSPICE CARE*

Children's Hospice is a concept of care for children and adolescents in the final stages of a life-threatening condition. Hospice care can take place anywhere—in the patient's home, in the hospital, or in other appropriate locations. In hospice care, the use of the term patient may refer to the patient him/herself as well as the patient's immediate support system, be it family and/or any combination of significant others.

Pediatric hospice care is achieved by addressing and balancing the individual needs of the patient and those of the family. This includes the developmental, psychosocial, and spiritual as well as the physical aspects of care. Support of anticipatory grief begins at the time of referral. Bereavement support is provided to the family for a period of at least one year after the death of the child.

Services must include, but are not limited to, those of physician and nurse, psychosocial, spiritual, bereavement, and any additional services necessary for appropriate care of the patient and family. Registered nurse consultation must be made available 24 hours a day as needed by the patient and family.

Children's hospice care facilitates the participation of parents in assuming the role of primary caregiver and supports the inclusion of the patient and family in the decision-making process to the best of their ability and commensurate with their desires. The hospice team supports the patient and family. In turn, the hospice team support is provided through scheduled access to ongoing education and training programs appropriate to their responsibilities to maintain skills necessary for the physical and psychosocial care of patients.

*Children's Hospice International, March 1985. Reprinted by permission.

10

INTERDISCIPLINARY TEAM

On a daily basis members of many disciplines interact with their hospice counterparts. The ideal relationship is one in which each member of the team channels the care and concern of his or her colleagues in the community into the hospice care-giving process.

Such community interrelationships are presented in the diagram on page 43. The team roles and the functions of team members are described below.

Interdisciplinary Team	Community Caring
Medicine	*Community Physicians*

In order to achieve certification, accreditation, or licensure, hospices are required to employ physicians, but only in the larger hospice programs would such professionals be employed full time. Hospice physicians direct efforts toward pain and symptom management, accept or reject patients on the basis of clearly defined admission criteria, and work with the members of the other disciplines, on a constantly changing basis, to revise and update the patient/family care plan.

Community physicians maintain primary patient relationships except in the case of a hospice inpatient service with its own staff of physicians.

Nursing *VNA/Hospital Nurses*

Because patients come into hospice care with a wide variety of symptoms, nursing care is essen-tial. In the home care setting the hospice nurse makes regularly scheduled visits, the frequency depending on the patient's condition. It is essential that nurses be available twenty-four hours a day, seven days a week to make house calls. In the inpatient setting a staff-patient ratio should be commensurate with the needs of the patients; the public health code in one state, Connecticut, places that at a 1:3 staff ratio around the clock, with one registered nurse for every six patients.

Hospital nurses frequently care for patients during long periods of hospitalization that precede hospice care. VNA nurses frequently care for patients before referral to hospice, either directly as part of hospice coverage or within a community coalition framework.

Pastoral Care *Community Clergy*

A pastoral care person is included on the interdisciplinary team as a hospice employee or a hospice volunteer. In addition to the provision of direct pastoral care services when these are appropriate, the pastoral care director tries at every point to enable and facilitate the involvement of community clergy in the care of their own parishioners.

Social Work *Community Social Workers*

A hospice social worker provides essential counseling care and seeks to work with patients and their families on matters that involve family deci-

Diagram of Hospice Interrelationship

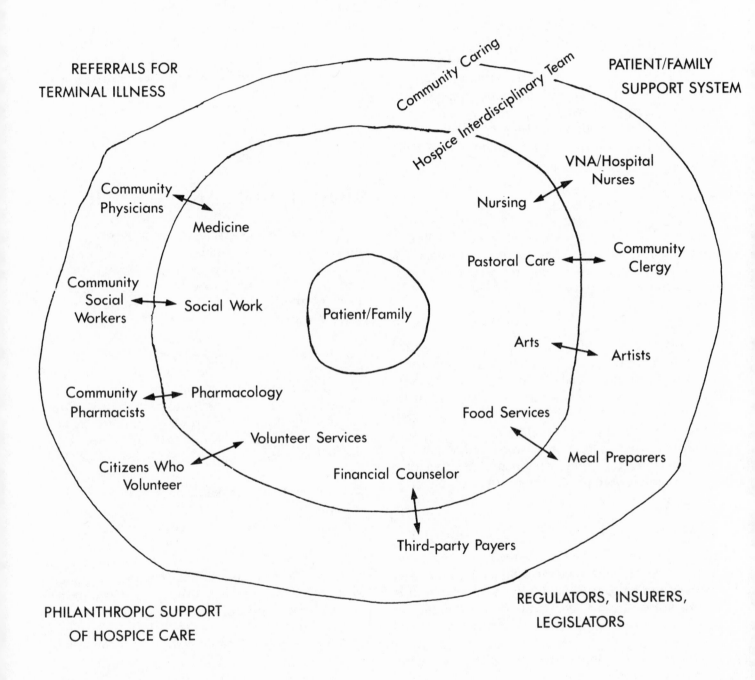

REFERRALS FOR TERMINAL ILLNESS

PATIENT/FAMILY SUPPORT SYSTEM

Community Caring

Hospice Interdisciplinary Team

Community Physicians → Medicine

VNA/Hospital Nurses ← Nursing

Community Social Workers ↔ Social Work

Pastoral Care ↔ Community Clergy

Patient/Family

Arts ↔ Artists

Community Pharmacists ↔ Pharmacology

Food Services

Volunteer Services

Meal Preparers

Citizens Who Volunteer

Financial Counselor

Third-party Payers

PHILANTHROPIC SUPPORT OF HOSPICE CARE

REGULATORS, INSURERS, LEGISLATORS

sion-making, children, and special problems such as alcoholism, AIDS, and marital stress. Community social workers frequently refer their patients to a hospice from a hospital or agency setting.

Pharmacology

Community Pharmacists

The use of pharmacological expertise in providing the most helpful and efficient medications for pain and symptom management has become a vital part of hospice care. The active presence of an interested community pharmacist is often essential in carrying out the principles of hospice care.

Arts   Artists

The arts represent a vital source of fulfillment in the quest of patients and families for quality of life. Going beyond traditional therapeutic roles, hospice arts programs use musicians, graphic artists, metalsmiths, writers, movement specialists, and many other artistic disciplines in enhancing the legacies that patients will leave to members of their families and in providing fulfillment for the basic goals of life.

Food Services   Meal Preparers

Many hospice patients, who have grown unaccustomed to eating regularly because of the illness, find new interest in food as the result of meals that incorporate taste, nutrition, and palatability with the aesthetic and artistic.

Volunteer Services   Citizens Who Volunteer

Hospice care would not be possible without a tremendous number of volunteers, whose service extends beyond the call of duty and who work in hospice because they want to. Hospice volunteers fulfill essential roles in enlarging the options open to patients and families as well as in supportive and administrative functions. Each volunteer should have a specific job description and be part of a built-in network of programmatic or administrative functions.

Financial Counselor   Third-party Payers

Working one's way through the intricacies of insurance coverage, Medicare, Blue Cross, and other carriers can be confusing at best. A knowledgeable counselor can assist most patients and families to discover resources and work through financial problems.

The "Four Corners of Hospice Care" are represented by the following:

1. The referrals that come from the community. They represent continuity in a time of frightful change.
2. The patient/family's own support system, which may be large in some instances and small in others. On occasion it may reach into every corner of the community's life.

3. Regulators, insurers, legislators,—the public sector, which, in the last analysis, makes possible the credibility of hospice care.
4. Philanthropic support, which provides for quality, assures continuity, and in fact makes hospice care possible. Third-party payers will never completely support a hospice program; planned methods for securing the philanthropic dollar are essential.

HOW THE TEAM FUNCTIONS

An interdisciplinary team consists of a group of health care professionals, representing different disciplines, who meet together regularly to plan for and work on hospice care. As the team members meet regularly, they develop a sense of profound trust in one another.

As noted earlier (page 20) considerable role-blurring takes place within the team. Whereas a visitor to a team meeting might expect that a physician would primarily speak to medical issues, a nurse to nursing issues, and a pastor to pastoral care issues, such is not the case. Each team member seeks to enhance the total care of the patient, and every discipline becomes an advocate for other disciplines.

Team sessions are based on a principle of absolute confidentiality, a fact that limits the participation of those who are not regular members of the team.

Care plans are discussed for those who are currently in the program, admissions of new patients to the progam are considered, and developments in a patient's condition since the last team meeting are reported.

The team concept moves from an early, tentative reaching out for understanding of what hospice care is, through a process of growth and developing awareness, to a finely tuned collegial way of dealing with patient and family care. The hospice interdisciplinary team is totally antithetical to a traditional medical model, in which the physician is in charge of caring for the patient and members of other disciplines take their orders accordingly. Rather, it is democratic, with the patient at the center.

INTERDISCIPLINARY CARE UNIQUE HOSPICE FEATURE*

Like a tapestry woven with many different threads, care by The Connecticut Hospice is an interplay of the skills of many different professions. Within hospice home and inpatient care, physicians, nurses, pharmacist, social workers, clergy, artists, volunteers, and consultants actively assist each patient and family in resolving the myriad difficulties surrounding terminal illness. It is this "team" approach—comprehensive, coordinated palliative care without gaps or overlaps—that truly distinguishes hospice within the health care system.

Notes Carol Yoder, R.N., Vice-President for Home Care: "The end result of quality care and the interdisciplinary approach is the ability to meet many areas of need for patients and families and help them work out situations that may have been problematic in the past. It may be in the area of physical discomfort, changes in appearance, religion, or patient-family relationships. The ability to help them resolve these problems demonstrates the high quality of care that we are able to bring to patients and families."

The hospice interdisciplinary team helps the patient and family to build a framework around which they learn to cope with and accept the realities of terminal illness. "The doctor and nurse are a close working team in hospice," says William Braisted, M.D., hospice physician. "We have a closer relationship than you might find in other health care settings."

In the inpatient building each day begins with morning reports and chart rounds. At this time nurses, physicians, and pharmacist discuss medication regimens, pain and other symptom control, and other issues related to patient care. After reviewing each patient's chart the physician begins morning rounds on each patient.

These daily meetings of the nurse, physician, and other members of the team assure

*From 1984 annual report of The Connecticut Hospice. Used with permission.

coordinated care. The weekly interdisciplinary team conferences contribute to resolving problems and plan care for the patient and family. In this way team members learn from one another and reinforce one another's strengths. Team members also assess and refer patients to other disciplines as the need arises.

The primary nurse initially assesses the patient and identifies problems and needs to be addressed. Because terminal illness has many ramifications, team care also includes the family. The nurse develops a custom-designed care plan and presents this to the rest of the interdisciplinary team. This occurs in both the home care and the inpatient programs.

The pharmacist is relied on to provide patients and families with drug information, patient monitoring, and patient counseling. An individualized approach to the design of all patients' drug regimens takes into account the unique characteristics and problems of each patient.

Pastoral caregivers provide spiritual support, as requested, with respect for individual values and beliefs. They work closely with community clergy whenever possible to assess the patient and family for religious history and the ability to be supportive at this time.

Social work is an integral part of the team approach. Hospice social workers help patients and families to bridge communication breakdowns and to grow with the reality of terminal illness. They also help to arrange community and financial supports. The bereavement program, which offers support to the grieving family for up to one year, is coordinated by the social work department.

Hospice care affirms life and focuses on the quality of life. To this end, hospice embraces and views the arts as an important component of care.

As members of the team, artists assist patients and families in individual creative projects. They hold performances, coordinate changing arts exhibits, and tend flowers and plants inside the building and in outside patio gardens.

The presence of children at hospice, through the Charlie Mills Preschool, enhances the atmosphere. The mix of staff, patients, patient families, and children benefits all parties. Adults respond with smiles as they see the children making their rounds through the building. The quality of life is enriched for everyone—children and adults.

The dietary department works closely with other members of the team to provide balanced, appealing menus for patients in the inpatient program and advice to families who are caring for terminally ill patients at home.

Volunteers participate in both direct patient care and support functions at hospice. Lay and professional volunteers provide a variety of services as part of the interdisciplinary team. They are a "someone like me" to the patient and family—a listening ear, a friendly visitor, a fresh perspective—in a difficult time.

Hospice does not take a narrow view of complexities of the needs of patients with a terminal illness and their families. Although the control of physical pain and other physical symptoms is the central and primary concern for caregivers, it is not the only priority. The terminally ill patient suffers from an array of emotional, spiritual, social, and financial problems.

The rationale for hospice caregiving is that it is impossible for any one discipline to provide the range of services required. Through the team approach, hospice helps patients and families to attain optimum quality of life.

11

PHYSICIAN CARE AND HOSPICE

Physicians carry a unique responsibility. For their patients they are a repository of medical knowledge. In many cases they symbolize a continuity of care for families over a long period. Some people have a special kind of confidence in the family doctor who has seen them through one illness after another, both in and out of hospitals. Others have a more tenuous relationship with the medical community, whom they know from visits to clinics or neighborhood walk-in medical centers.

The inauguration of hospice care at a particular time in a patient's life requires physician approval. The time when that referral takes place is of great importance, for it determines the extent to which the interdisciplinary team may begin to do its work and achieve the comfort the patient requires.

A bereaved family member whose father died in a hospice program described a not-unusual feeling:

> About four months before my father's death, his physician abandoned him. We had known the doctor socially, and he had told me that he has problems telling patients and their families that the illness is terminal. For four months he did not set foot in the house. But what made me angry was the fact that when he was asked if he would be prepared to make the pronouncement, he agreed. He would come when my father was dead but not while he was alive.

Local committees studying hospice care will want to assess the level of physician involvement in the hospice program. In an effort to better analyze the physician's role, two physicians on the staff of The Connecticut Hospice were asked several questions. Participants were Robert P. Zanes, M.D., Vice-President for Medical Affairs of The Connecticut Hospice and the organization's medical director, and Carl Osier, M.D., Staff Physician.

How do you feel that physicians, as a whole, handle a prognosis of a terminal illness with their patients?

DR. ZANES: Over long years of practice I have observed that physicians, as a whole, have difficulty when their patients are dying. To begin with, physicians are uncomfortable telling a patient of a diagnosis of cancer, but they do it. The ones that have to, such as oncologists, have become good at that, mainly because they can hold out the hope of what treatment can be provided. But when aggressive therapy is not appropriate, they have difficulty in telling a patient that everything that can be done has been done and that from that point on the physician's job is to make them comfortable.

Is it then a "death is defeat" syndrome?

DR. OSIER: From day one, physicians are trained to cure. If you cure, you succeed. If you don't cure, you fail at some level, and if your patient dies, it is an absolute failure. Death is absolute failure. Nobody who has been successful, and wishes to continue to be successful, wants to face that.

Does not the principle of palliation, as opposed to cure, offer profound hope to physicians in what they have to offer their patients?

DR. ZANES: The average physician in the community is not ready to say that there is a time to switch from aggressive care to palliative care. A missionary in the community could convince local physicians that palliative care can be effective if, as in the case of good pain and symptom management, it is properly applied. The physician needs to know that this can be done in the home, and that it can be done without the physician abandoning or giving up his or her patient.

Apart from the major medical centers and teaching institutions, how does the medical community view hospice?

DR. OSIER: Some physicians see hospice as merely hand-holding. And they think that the concept of the interdisciplinary team is a threat. They feel pushed aside and usurped in their role. Physicians have not received enough training to enable them to rely on a team model.

How do physicians respond to the hospice emphasis on quality of life?

DR. ZANES: In hospice one realizes that time is not important and that it is the quality that counts. But many physicians are so busy with all the other important things that they do not have time for quality until they come to hospice.

What would you say about the ethical issue raised by some critics who feel that the use of morphine could contribute to a patient's death?

DR. ZANES: What such critics are talking about is the fact that according to the books, morphine is supposed to suppress respirations. More of our patients have lung cancer than any other diagnosis, so respiration is important. But our experience has been that morphine does not suppress respirations; it relaxes, and in fact it is used in the treatment of respiratory distress. We carefully titrate the dosages in order that the patient may be alert.

What is the most effective way of persuading community physicians to be supportive of hospice?

DR. OSIER: The most effective way would be for patients in the community to go to their own physicians—in other words, to known, trusted people—and say, "I am interested in hospice" and ask, "Where are you on hospice?"

How can a local physician become involved most helpfully in areas where there is no available program?

DR. OSIER: The energy needs to go into opening doors and opening minds. The concerned physician can become the center of a nucleus group. A doctor who does his or her reading about hospice, who goes to a hospice conference, or who comes to The Connecticut Hospice for technical assistance, can then gather peers around to share in exploration. Community or regional networking can be helpful also.

THE FUTURE OF PHYSICIAN INVOLVEMENT—A CONCERN

A hospice administrator on the West Coast* writes:

> I think physicians, oncologists in particular, are again beginning to advocate aggressive therapy when there is little rationale, e.g., routinely offering total parenteral nutrition to very terminal patients. Personally, I think their motivation is to recapture dollars that have been lost in other areas of their practice.

Recent events highlight a number of major issues for physicians centering around how they are paid for their services. Many physicians routinely charge their patients for hospital visits. Yet the adoption of the DRG (diagnosis-related group) method of payment, first by Medicare and then by others, limits the hospital stays of patients, and therefore the number of visits for which charges may be made. (In the DRG method hospitals are paid for illnesses rather than for length of stay.) Increasing numbers of physicians are suing group insurance providers, such as Blue Cross, in several states for insufficient payment to them.

*Claire Tehan, Vice-President for Hospice, Hospital Home Health Care Agency of California, in personal correspondence with the editor.

Hospice care stresses the right of the patient and family to decide to discontinue treatment when it is unlikely to produce healing results, or when quality of life is more important than length. This decision does clearly limit the physician's potential for income, although it enhances the physician-patient relationship from the standpoint of humanitarian concern for the feelings of all involved.

The local congregation, of which patients and their families may well be members, is in an ideal position to act, on one hand, as a watchdog on trends of physician concern for hospice care and, on the other, as an advocate for the terminally ill and their right for decision irrespective of what their physicians may desire.

EFFECTIVE PAIN AND SYMPTOM MANAGEMENT—RESULT OF MEDICAL AND PHARMACOLOGIC LEADERSHIP*

When Marie first came to hospice she suffered from a variety of symptoms—pain, nausea, sleeplessness, loss of appetite, anxiety—all related to her end-stage breast cancer. In addition, Marie worried about the future of her three teenage children and her husband. The family faced economic hardships imposed by her illness. And they struggled with deep, spiritual questions about dying and death.

At hospice, Marie found a comprehensive program of pain and symptom control that recognized the interplay between physical pain and a patient's emotional, psychological, spiritual, and financial needs.

The spirit of hospice is to encourage quality of existence for patients and families. Because of this abiding philosophy, pain and symptom control lie at the very heart of the hospice program of care. Medical and pharmacological therapies control a range of debilities that, if untreated, sap a patient's strength, will, even human dignity.

Professional expertise and an individualized care plan make possible a control of pain seldom achieved in other health care settings. Nowhere is this more evident than in the work of the hospice physician, nurse, and pharmacist.

"There are multiple possible causes for the various symptoms which develop in a person during the end stage of terminal illness," says Robert P. Zanes, M.D., Medical Director of

*From 1984 annual report of The Connecticut Hospice. Used with permission.

The Connecticut Hospice. Zanes, formerly Chief of the Hematology-Oncology Section and Director of the Oncology Unit at Hospital of Saint Raphael, New Haven, Connecticut, is an Associate Professor of Clinical Medicine at the Yale University School of Medicine. "Flexibility is an important attitude in assessing treatment methodologies."

The physician, pharmacist, and nurse are important team members in evaluating pain and treating it pharmacologically. Artists, social workers, clergy, nurses, and professional and lay volunteers work with psychological and spiritual pain. As a team, they review the patient's status daily. In addition, consultants in several fields of health care complement the efforts of the medical and nursing staffs. In evaluating Marie the hospice physician was supported in his diagnosis by other members of the team.

Patients seek hospice care for many reasons. Like Marie, approximately 95 percent of hospice patients have cancer. Yet the disease categories for hospice admission also include end-stage lung, kidney, and cardiac disease; Huntington's chorea; and amyotrophic lateral sclerosis (Lou Gehrig's disease). The criteria for admission remain constant: prognosis is limited (usually six months or less) and palliative care is accepted.

Before admitting a patient to the hospice program, the hospice physician confers with the family's physician, and they retain open lines of communication. In the home care program the family's physician acts as the primary physician and the role of the hospice physician varies from case to case. In the inpatient unit the hospice physician assumes the primary physician role. In both programs medical direction is available twenty-four hours a day.

The care plan must be creative, innovative, and flexible to respond to the constantly changing challenges of terminal illness. Some symptoms can be relieved by simple measures, such as repositioning, massage, relaxation techniques, and distraction through arts and other activities. Yet medications are often crucial in alleviating physical discomfort.

In treating the patient the hospice physician and pharmacist are guided by repeated assessments, with adjustments in medications and times of administration so that the patient can be as comfortable as possible.

"The involvement of the pharmacist is crucial and much greater here than in other health care settings," says The Connecticut Hospice's Director of Pharmacy, Anne Steitz. "Because our patients are so ill, their medication regimens are usually fairly complicated. The cases are very involved and require that the pharmacist have a much greater grasp of the various drugs and their dosages."

An important principle in the hospice approach is that drug dosages are carefully adjusted to each patient's physical makeup. This assures pain relief without a loss of alertness. The hospice goal is to control symptoms while maintaining optimum functioning.

"Every patient's drug regimen is individualized," Anne Steitz explains. "Every patient has factors that impact on the care plan, such as compromised renal function, dehydration, and malnutrition. We design a drug regimen that takes these factors into account."

At hospice the patient's needs dictate the medication level. Medications are administered on a regular schedule to eliminate not only pain, but also the fear of pain. "We do not want patients to wait until they are in pain," Dr. Zanes says. "That only produces tension and anxiety, both of which make the pain worse."

Ease of administration is a key consideration as well. Patients are spared injections whenever possible to make their lives more comfortable. More than 90 percent of the medications at hospice are taken orally. Because of this it is often possible for patients to be cared for at home.

When a medication is not available commercially in the exact dosage needed, the pharmacist prepares this to meet individual needs. An active participant in patient care, the pharmacist attends morning rounds and weekly team meetings, serving as a source of current drug information and as a consultant for changing drug regimens.

Both the hospice pharmacist and the physician strive to educate others on the goals and parameters of hospice caregiving. This year the number of requests for technical assistance spiraled. Both Robert Zanes and Anne Steitz joined other team members in presenting a seminar in Montreal on the impact of difficult and complex family situations on symptom control, and they discussed symptom control protocols in a seminar at the National Hospice Organization annual meeting.

A palliative task force of nurses, physicians, and pharmacist at The Connecticut Hospice is working on the development of a manual on symptom control protocols.

Advances in symptom control present diversified and constant challenges. As the hospice physician and pharmacist discharge their demanding duties, they are in the forefront of palliative care. Hospice remains identified by its excellence of symptom management and support.

12

HOSPICE DYNAMICS— HOW DOES IT WORK?

Members of the local church first need to understand how the local hospice program functions in order to facilitate and participate in hospice care. Hospice care functions quite differently from area to area and from community to community largely because the concept of hospice has been applied in a number of ways.

Basically there are four organizational models; each of these has a number of variations. Terminology used to describe these models varies, but the most essential factors relate to where the basic authority lies for carrying out the hospice program. From this "locus" perspective, hospice programs may be categorized as follows.

1. *Home Health Agency Model.* The program is centered on the Visiting Nurse Association or a similar public health nursing agency. It may consist entirely of home care carried on by members of the staff of the agency, or there may be a contractual relationship with a hospital, nursing home, or other facility for the offering of inpatient care. Later in this chapter the program of the Columbia-Montour Home Health Agency of Bloomsburg, Pennsylvania, is described in detail.

2. *Hospital-based Model.* The program is centered within the organizational structure of a com-

munity or other hospital. Appropriate inpatient care is provided in a hospice unit located in the hospital itself or through a "scatter bed" approach in which hospice patients are cared for within other units of the hospital by a hospice team. Home care may be provided by the hospital's home care department or through a contract with a local visiting nurse association, or in some instances it may not be available. The hospice program of the Abbott-Northwestern Hospital Hospice of Minneapolis, Minnesota, is described later.

3. *Independent Model.* The program is carried on by an independent organization, usually incorporated expressly for this purpose. The hospice may be only a home care program, or a home care program with contractual relationships with a local hospital for inpatient care. Or the independent hospice may operate its own home care and inpatient programs, with a full continuum of care under its own auspices. The latter approach is described in the pages that follow through the description of The Connecticut Hospice of Branford, Connecticut.

4. *Coalition Model.* The hospice program itself has minimal staff or, in some instances, perhaps no paid staff. Basic care is provided by visiting nurse

51

associations, hospitals, or other caregiving entities in the community or region. This model is presented here with a description of the Hospice of the Upper Valley of Lebanon, New Hampshire.

The following tables describe the differences among the four models:

RESPONSIBILITY OR AUTHORITY BY MODEL

Loci of Authority	Authority	Whose Staff?	Medically Directed	24 Hours a Day
Hospital	Hospital trustees	Employs its own for inpatient care. May have its own home care staff, or contract	Yes	Yes
Home health	VNA board	Employs its own. Contract for inpatient care	May have consultant	Yes for home care. Inpatient care depends on contract.
Independent	Own board of directors	Own staff for home care. May have own inpatient unit or contract	Yes	Yes
Coalition	Community board	Small central staff, mostly from community agencies	Depends on local community	Yes

Base may be anywhere. See definitions page 51.

HOSPICE CONTINUUM ACCORDING TO MODEL

	HOME CARE	INPATIENT CARE	BEREAVEMENT CARE
Hospital-based	May have its own or contract in community	Own; hospice unit or scatter bed	May have its own or depend on local community
Home health agency	Does its own	Contract with hospital or other setting	May have its own or depend on local community
Independent	Own	May operate its own or contract	Does its own
Coalition	Carried on by community agencies	Carried on by nearby hospital	Does its own

Base may be anywhere. See definitions page 51.

	HOSPITAL	HOME HEALTH AGENCY	INDEPENDENT	COALITION
Medical	On staff	Contract, on staff, or none	On staff	Depends on community
Nursing	On staff for inpatient care; may contract for home care	On staff	On staff	Community agencies
Social work	On staff	On staff	May be on staff	Community
Pastoral care	On staff	Depends on volunteers	May be staff or volunteer	Community volunteer
Volunteer coordinator	On staff	May be on staff	On staff	May be on central coordinating staff

The following case studies of the four models are presented to encourage further understanding of the hospice program.

Freestanding or Independent Model: The Connecticut Hospice, Inc., Branford, Connecticut

Rosemary J. Hurzeler, R.N., M.P.H., H.A., President

In the beginning nobody wanted us. It was not because the idea wasn't compelling, but because it was *fragile*. To integrate it into existing systems could have broken it. All those involved, principals and advisers alike, wanted a *hospice* and sought an environment that would allow it to be nurtured and to become an effective instrument of caring.

Those leaders had a gut feeling that a separate place and ethos were needed, a place and ethos that could inspire, create, and maintain their integrity. Perhaps it was far from realistic back then—and a bit impractical. But nonetheless the experience of The Connecticut Hospice—and between 1980 and 1986 we have seen more than 7,500 patients and families—is that those original

feelings were correct. A *free*standing hospice works.

Maybe it starts with the word free—free to *be* free, free from other competing interests, free to devote all one's time to *one* thing, free to have a place people can put their arms around to feel "hospice," free to demonstrate in a closed system the benefits of palliative care.

But it was Milton Friedman who said that there is no free lunch, and perhaps that is true for hospice; there is no such thing as "free"-standing. Everything about it costs. Economies of scale are not there, but one's identity is so clear that patients and families, staff, volunteers, and the philanthropic community pay one back for the courage and the grace to stand alone.

The Connecticut Hospice, founder of American hospice care, is an independent nonprofit corporation that employs a staff of 195, including home care nurses, and inpatient nursing staff sufficient to provide a ratio of one nursing staff member for every three patients twenty-four hours a day, and an interdisciplinary team of physicians, social workers, clergy, an arts coordinator, a clinical pharmacist, and a food service director, in addition to the nurses and the administrative and support personnel.

The Hospice operates a home care program that serves eighteen towns and cities in the Greater New Haven area and a forty-four-bed specialty hospice hospital that serves patients from all over Connecticut. During 1985 1,100 patients were served, 193 receiving home care only, 712 inpatient care only, and 196 a combination of inpatient and home care.

The Connecticut Hospice is licensed by the state of Connecticut as a "short-term hospital, special, hospice" and is certified by Medicare as a hospice. It is accredited by the Joint Commission on the Accreditation of Hospitals.

REFERRAL

The caregiving process begins with a referral telephone call, which may come from a variety of sources, including physicians, hospitals, visiting nurse associations, local clergy, or the patient's own family.

Physicians and hospital discharge planners both play a significant role in the process: physicians because, before a patient may be received into care, their assessment of the prognosis is required and discharge planners because, at the time of referral, many patients are still hospitalized after undergoing various curative procedures.

Some 497 physicians made referrals during a five-year period. If the initial call is not from a physician, The Connecticut Hospice admission counselor will call the patient's doctor for the patient's history and for more information.

HOME CARE

If the patient is a candidate for the home care program, a home care nurse will visit the home and make an assessment visit to determine whether the needs of the patient and family are such that they could be served in the hospice program. If the services of a home health aide or homemaker are required, they may be secured as the result of contractual arrangements with several visiting nurse associations or other private-duty health care agencies.

A home care nurse will schedule regular visits to the home on the basis of the patient's condition. However, through a twenty-four-hour answering service, a home care nurse is always available to make house calls at any time of the day or night.

When a home care patient requires inpatient admission, this can easily be arranged, thus demonstrating the home care/inpatient continuum that is so important to hospice care.

Within the home care program the patient's own physician maintains the primary physician relationship; The Connecticut Hospice staff physicians play an advisory role. On some occasions, at the request of the patient's physician, a hospice physician may make a house call.

A social worker, artist, or other team member may become involved in the patient/family situation if the need arises. In many cases one or more volunteers will be involved in the home setting to provide transportation, stay with the patient so that family members may get out of the house, assist with shopping, or whatever may be required. A care coordinator makes sure that everything that is needed is made available at the appropriate time.

INPATIENT CARE

The inpatient building, which was especially designed for hospice care, serves as an essential backup that makes hospice home care viable. Inpatient admission, usually expressly for pain and symptom management, comes during the last stages of an illness; average length of stay is fourteen days, with more than half the patients remaining no longer than eight days. Hospice inpatient care is therefore based on the premise that terminally ill patients are quite sick and therefore require considerable and constant attention from a dedicated and highly professional staff. A staff of physicians constantly monitors the condition of patients both in one-on-one visits and during daily rounds, along with nurse and pharmacist representation.

The Connecticut public health code for hospice licensure requires a 1:3 nursing staff-patient ratio twenty-four hours a day and 1:6 registered nurse-patient ratio. When compared with traditional health care settings, this gives members of the nursing staff time to work with family members as well as with patients. The willingness of a hospice nurse to listen, be it in the daytime or the middle of the night, adds much to the unique spirit of the hospice building.

The environment of inpatient care includes ample space for families and friends, room for personal possessions, and twenty-four-hour visiting privileges with no discrimination against children, infants, or pets. Patients and their families have many caregiving options available to them, including participation in the arts.

Approximately 15 percent of patients are discharged for care in the home or in another health care facility. Whenever possible such arrangements in the home are carried out through either the organization's own home care program or a hospice home care program in another part of the state. Discharges are basically the result of the institution of effective pain and symptom management, and the discovery of a level of medication that may be carried on in the home, or the fact that the condition of the patient no longer requires such intensive around-the-clock intervention by the hospice staff.

BEREAVEMENT

A volunteer bereavement team, coordinated by a social worker, provides continuing bereavement care for families for a year after the death of the patient whenever required.

PRESCHOOL

Child care is integrated with patient care through a licensed preschool for three- and four-year-old children of staff and community. This attention to the early years of life, in the midst of a setting devoted to the end of life, truly represents a continuum that demonstrates the importance of quality of life for as long as it lasts.

Hospital-based Hospice: Abbott-Northwestern Hospital Hospice, Minneapolis, Minnesota

Howard K. Bell, M. Div., Coordinator for Hospice Care

Hospice is a concept of care that can be applied in a multitude of settings. The concept implies care that is directed at palliation and comfort measures rather than at curative or life-prolonging measures. Having a patient, family, and health care team jointly understand, support, and commit themselves to this concept creates hospice, rather than administrative structures. To make the concept a reality a service must be developed and standards of care adhered to. There is nearly universal acceptance of the standards as developed by the National Hospice Organization. These standards identify the key principles that are required to advance the hospice concept in any setting.

An essential element of hospice care is the commitment of individuals who bring the hospice concept of care to people who are in need of it. These unique individuals may appear within any setting and are characterized as follows:

- Individuals who recognize that there is a time to say "enough is enough"
- Individuals who can accept and confront death as a natural part of life and not as a "failure"
- Individuals who are committed to working on an interdisciplinary team to combat any symptom of pain, discomfort or distress
- Individuals who perceive the wholistic nature of people as composed of physical, psychosocial, and spiritual dimensions
- Individuals who are committed to caring as deeply as they are committed to curing
- Individuals who can embrace the families of patients no matter how broken, divided, or nontraditional
- Individuals willing to support the bereaved through their time of loss

All models of hospice care must be defined by quality standards and committed individuals. As a hospital-based model we may be required to work more diligently, since we are attempting to apply the concept in an essentially "hostile" environment. The hospital is the bastion of technology and of professional codes of life preservation. People are motivated and rewarded for competencies that are quite different from those required by the hospice concept. The setting is highly institutionalized, and schedules are tailored more to the professionals' needs than to those of the patients and families.

The rationale for hospitals to operate a hospice program has been multifaceted. The primary commitment has been to provide a full continuum of care. Integration of hospice with the cure-oriented aggressive care that precedes it allows for patients to maintain continuity with their physicians, health care team members, and health care facilities. The fear of abandonment is reduced. The patient and family can take comfort from the earliest stage of diagnosis and treatment that they will continue to be cared for even when cure is no longer possible.

Hospitals have also been motivated to have a hospice service as a marketing tool, especially for a comprehensive cancer center. This has been true despite the fact that hospice reimbursement has been less than the total operating costs. Since the early 1980s, competition among hospitals has increasingly influenced programmatic decisions. A final rationale is a recognition of the appropriateness as well as the ultimate cost-effectiveness of hospice service.

Abbott-Northwestern Hospital made a decision in 1979 to initiate planning for a hospice program to be an integral part of its comprehensive cancer program. There were already ten other hospital-based hospice programs operating in the Twin Cities Metropolitan Area. The hospice was intended primarily to serve those patients already being treated by Abbott-Northwestern Hospital. A decision was made to designate six beds on a forty-four-bed oncology unit for inpatient hospice care. This meant that utilization would be based on hospital acute-care criteria and that reimbursement would be for hospital care rather than uniquely for hospice. The designated beds prioritized for hospice also meant that patients could be cared for by specially trained nurses rather than having hospice patients scattered throughout the hospital. These designated beds could then be used by other patients if they were not filled by hospice patients. This flexible arrangement has both benefits and drawbacks. The benefits are primarily in the area of cost savings. Beds do not have to be left open for potential revenue loss. Staffing can be integrated within a larger unit. There is an infiltration of the hospice philosophy and practices into the traditional care setting. The drawbacks are primarily in the area of compromise of hospice idealism. The homelike setting is minimalized. Staffing control remains outside of hospice. There is a limited sense of "community." The inpatient unit feels very much like the rest of the hospital.

As indicated, the hospital-based hospice tends to serve patients and families who are already served by the hospital. This arrangement en-

hances physician participation, since the physician is able to continue in the primary role. Our medical director role has been minimal. He has approved protocols, consults with team members as needed, problem solves with attending M.D.s at the request of the team, is available for patient consultation when requested, and will assume attending physician responsibilities for referrals from outside our system. Physicians have become strong supporters of our program as an extension of their care. They appreciate the resources of the team members, particularly their availability to work with difficult families. They refer, easily knowing that they will not need to alter their established relationship and that there will be the least disruption of the caregiving setting.

Home care is still the hallmark of the hospital-based hospice. There is a commitment to provide the necessary services to enable a patient to be cared for and die at home if that is his or her desire. A primary careperson who is able and willing to provide for the comfort needs of the patient at home is required. Resources are also available for extended hours of professional help at home. Medicare reimbursement to hospitals through diagnosis-related groups (DRGs) have pressed hospices toward home care utilization more than the 80/20 cap provision of the Medicare hospice benefit. Even though we have elected not to become Medicare-certified, our percentage of days have averaged significantly more than 80 percent under home hospice care.

Our home hospice care is managed through our own hospital-based home care agency. On hospital discharge a hospice patient is technically referred to home health. All billing for home hospice services is done through home health under traditional home care reimbursement, rather than uniquely as hospice services. The patient is actively followed by the hospital-based interdisciplinary team. This follow-up includes weekly phone calls, the availability of trained volunteers, weekly interdisciplinary team meetings for review of care, coordination of spiritual services through the hospital chaplain and local clergy, and social work services. None of these services are billed to the patient, nor is reimbursement sought. Specially trained nurses serve as the primary support for patients and families in their homes. They visit as required and are available on-call twenty-four hours a day, seven days a week.

The hospice volunteer program is similarly integrated within the hospital volunteer service. There is a part-time paid coordinator. All record-keeping and supportive services are provided through the volunteer department. There are three hospice volunteer components: inpatient services, home care services, and bereavement services. All volunteers attend special training and are required to document hours and patient/family interactions. The coordinator attends team meetings and makes appropriate matches as well as oversees follow-up accountability. At least quarterly support or educational activities are held in addition to one-on-one staff support. Each bereaved person is assessed as to need and resources by the chaplain and social worker, who serve as bereavement codirectors. A five-week grief support group is available. Individual volunteers are assigned to those in need of regular contact from the hospice program.

Clinical management for supportive care nursing interventions and patient care coordination is the responsibility of a full-time hospice clinical specialist. She advises and consults with physicians, patients and their families, and team members. She interfaces with inpatient nursing staff as well as home care nurses. She conducts the hospice assessment, introduces the program to patients and families, and obtains their consent. This unique role has permitted this position to be used as a most significant educational tool throughout the hospital system in the area of pain management. The hospice clinical specialist conducts seminars and lectures both within the professional community and for the general public.

The coordinator for hospice care is a full-time staff person who is engaged in about 50 percent administrative functions and about 50 percent counseling functions. He serves as the primary representative of the hospice to external groups, including receiver of outside referrals. He also conducts assessments and is a full-time member of the interdisciplinary team. He serves as a liaison to other hospital departments and provides programmatic direction and staff development. By being available to other hospital committees, he brings the hospice perspective to other hospital issues and concerns.

The hospital-based model for hospice care as practiced at Abbott-Northwestern is not presented as necessarily ideal. It illustrates how a high-quality hospice program could be structured and operated in a hospital setting. Each system might well need to adapt its operation to meet its own unique needs. The emphasis, however, must be on meeting quality standards, encouraging committed professionals, and allowing patient/family needs to dictate care. Concerned church members interacting with such programs in their communities need to find access to these people and to advocate for standards and practices of the highest quality of hospice care.

Home Health Agency Hospice: Columbia-Montour Home Health Services Visiting Nurse Association, Bloomsburg, Pennsylvania

Linda K. Baker, R.N., Coordinator of Special Services

Hospice care is provided by an interdisciplinary extended-care team, which consists of the extended-care staff, extended-care volunteers, the client and his or her family (who are the unit of care), the client's primary physician, and any cooperating community agencies that may be involved.

Of the terminally ill clients who are served by our Association, about 20 to 25 percent are cared for by the hospice team. The other 75 to 80 percent fall into one or more of the the following categories: denial of the terminality of the disease, death in a hospital or nursing home, refusal by the medical doctor to agree to hospice, or refusal of hospice care by the client or significant other.

Almost all our staff and front-line management nurses rotate onto the hospice team. This means that when the staff is not working with hospice clients, it is working with regular clients. Thus, during the ongoing relationship with those served by the agency, there are many occasions to discuss the subject of hospice care early on in the terminal stage of the disease process. Client, family members, and physician can then afford some time to think about hospice goals and options. We believe that having the nursing staff rotate on and off the hospital team broadens the client's options.

Entry into hospice care is as simple as someone saying to our agency, "I think this person could benefit from hospice." A hospice nurse then visits with the client and family to assess their understanding of and receptivity to the hospice concept. Once the client and significant other indicate a desire for hospice care in the home, the coordinator of special services contacts the client's physician.

Referrals come from hospital social workers, physicians, family members, friends, or the clients themselves, in that order. Most referrals are initiated on the telephone and are handled by the coordinator of special services, who is a registered nurse with hospice training and experience.

Each person handles the death and dying process differently. Therefore, each hospice client and family are unique in their needs and the level of care required to meet those needs.

The Columbia-Montour Home Health Services Visiting Nurse Association hospice team consists of an administrator, a medical director, a coordinator of special services, a team leader, a staff nurse, a social worker, a home health aide, and a volunteer. Physical therapy, occupational therapy, and speech therapy are provided by therapists who are specially trained and experienced in the area of hospice.

What a member of the hospice team will do with and for a client both physically and psychologically during any of the preceding stages depends on what the client wants and allows to happen. Skilled nursing visits can occur as often as two times a day, seven days a week, or as infrequently as every two weeks. The nurse may be there at the time of the client's death or may not be needed by the family and therefore be absent.

Social work visits are usually made two to three times a month but, again, can be as frequent as three times a week, depending on need. Physical therapy, occupational therapy, and speech therapy are often involved on an as-needed basis during the dying process. These three individual therapists support the quality of life, and often dying clients have something that they do just before their death. Helping them to accomplish their final earthly tasks is the goal of the therapists of our hospice team.

Home health aides can be used as often as once a day, seven days a week, or as little as once a week. Home health aides and volunteers are always initially taken into a home by the hospice nurses. Home health aide supervision is routinely performed every two weeks by one of the hospice nurses with the client and significant other supervision.

Volunteers usually serve as a relief person for the significant other; that is, they provide respite. The actual tasks that they perform in that role can vary widely, for example, reading to a client to changing a client's position in bed and doing skin care.

Through the bereavement component a member of our hospice team continues to work with the client's significant other for one year after the client's death.

Pastoral care is the weakest link in our hospice program for two reasons: (1) our hospice program cannot afford to have a pastoral care worker as a member of the official agency team, and (2) we cannot communicate with the client's minister, priest, or rabbi without the client's permission. Many clients refuse the team permission to talk or meet with their clergyperson. When a client grants permission for us to communicate, the team seeks information and shares and seeks support. The minister, priest, or rabbi can be as involved as he or she desires. If the clergyperson contacts the hospice team directly and we do not have the client's permission to share with him or her, we must so inform the minister, priest, or rabbi. We encourage that clergyperson to work with his or her parishioner on granting permission for communication.

There is no inpatient hospice unit or facility in our two counties. This negatively affects hospice in the home because we cannot offer the public the option of "The Dying Person's Bill of Rights" as an inpatient.

Our program is not certified under Medicare. To date this has not posed any problem for our hospice families that are covered under Medicare. The frightening problem is the plight of hospice families that are not covered under Medicare.

In 1985, 48 percent of our hospice caseload were under age sixty-five and not covered by Medicare. A large segment of the public that wants hospice is dying at a younger age, and the insurance industry does not meet that need. Our hospice clients who have no insurance coverage, or whose insurance coverage expires, have their hospice care costs met through our agency's hospice fund. The fund exists because consumers make donations to it. The fund is never so financially solvent that it does not need more contributions.

This leads me to comment on public awareness. We hear hospice families say over and over again, "I never knew you were here." Most people are not aware of hospice. Why? Because of lack of interest on their part and lack of public relations on the part of hospice groups. Church members should spread the word that hospice is here and ready and expensive. Money is needed for all types of hospice organizations, be they home-based, freestanding, or facility-based.

Community Coalition Model: Hospice of the Upper Valley, Lebanon, New Hampshire

Doreen Schweizer, M.S.W., Director

Hospice of the Upper Valley (HUV) is an autonomous agency that directs a volunteer program as well as an educational component. Serving twenty-two towns in Vermont and New Hampshire with a paid staff of three persons and an active, imaginative core of volunteers, the hospice program provides supplemental (non-medical) services and works with other existing health care agencies to deliver comprehensive care to terminally ill patients and their families. HUV, seven home health agencies (HHAs) one large teaching hospital, one Veteran's Administration hospital, and two smaller community hospitals constitute this informal coalition.

In describing the value of HUV in this network of care Mrs. R., an eighty-three-year-old woman whose husband had recently died, stated: "They cared about us. . . well, the others they cared, too, but Hospice, they *knew* about us. That's so important. . . that somebody knows about you." The HHA nurses and the staff at the hospital where her husband eventually died did an excellent job, and they did care; but the German-speaking volunteer who listened while Mr. R. reminisced about his youth in World War I and the young woman who visited and supported Mrs. R. and who often drove her to the hospital to visit her husband did more than care. They knew the story. They even lived a bit of it. In this way they helped Mr. and Mrs. R. to rebalance and find their

own meaning and comfort. After Mr. R.'s death Mrs. R attended the support group for recently bereaved people. She didn't talk much; she listened. Some time later she said, "I couldn't have made it without them . . . without Hospice. They helped me understand."

With so many caregivers involved, coordination and continuity of care are important issues. HUV sponsors an interdisciplinary team that consists of the hospice care coordinator (R.N.-nurse), the program coordinator (M.S.W-social work), the hospice medical adviser (M.D.), and a clergyperson (M.Div.), as well as the nursing supervisors of two of the HHAs and an oncologist from the teaching hopital; other caregivers are invited to case conferences when appropriate. In addition to its defined tasks of admitting patient/families to the program and developing and overseeing a care plan, the team often acts as patient advocate or case manager and ensures that the hospice philosophy is an integral part of care.

There are three paid staff. The care coordinator is responsible for carrying out the team's decisions: she visits prospective patients and families, assesses the possible relevance of hospice intervention, provides direction to the team in developing and overseeing a care plan, communicates with other caregivers, and involves volunteers and gives them ongoing backup support and guidance. The program coordinator is administrative director of the program and works closely with HUV's board of directors as well as with other agency directors in ongoing program maintenance and planning. She is responsible for the educational aspect of the program (the recruiting and training of volunteers, community programs, and in-service workshops for professionals). She also directs HUV's social work component, including the bereavement support group. A part-time office manager/bookkeeper/secretary assists in the details of overall program management.

A pool of fifty administrative and direct service volunteers is the heart of this hospice program, which encourages, but does not pressure, families to keep their loved ones at home to die. Volunteers are able to visit patients and families at home, where they can provide help with routine tasks such as meal preparation, transportation, personal care, as well as in area hospitals and nursing homes. Friendship, support, and guidance are assured to the patient/family unit throughout the illness and continue into the period of bereavement. A bereavement support group is available to these families and to other community members who have experienced a recent loss through death. Also, in conjunction with its lending library, which includes resource material on hospices throughout the United States, and its community awareness programs, HUV offers a consultation service to people who may have loved ones far away who are dying: again, support and guidance are given, and again, most important, hospice people listen to the story. In Mrs. R.'s words, "hospice knows about them."

HUV recognizes the spiritual tone of its work and the reality of its role in pastoral care, and relationships with local parishes and area clergy are particularly important to the agency. Community ministers and the hospital chaplains help with volunteer training and have pointed out the unique position of the volunteers as pastoral caregivers: they don't carry the expectations and fears that are often projected onto clergy. Many of the volunteers have strong church relationships through which they find strength and support. Some parishes have been especially active in de-

veloping educational programs designed to raise church members' consciousness of death and grief and of other issues related to hospice care. Many church groups have made financial contributions to HUV; such donations are important to the continuance of the program.

An ongoing concern for HUV is funding. Its services are not included in any government or private insurance coverage because they do not fit current definitions of reimbursable services; and although the other agencies in the coalition depend on HUV's volunteers, its interdisciplinary team, and its bereavement and education programs, they have not as yet been able to offer financial support. The board of directors (volunteers) takes the primary responsibility for fundraising. Currently 68 percent of the approximately $50,000 budget comes from private contributions in a direct-mail fund appeal and from memorial donations, with the rest coming from special events, a few small grants and seven towns in the catchment area. This support has kept the agency alive and affirms the value of hospice care to this community.

13

THE SEARCH FOR STANDARDS

The use of the word hospice, unfortunately, does not assure the maintenance, in every state, of minimum hospice standards. Yet standards are crucial if patients and their families are to be able to achieve genuine quality of life and if care is to be commensurate with the needs of the patients (see chapter 4).

The National Hospice Organization (NHO) adopted standards for hospice care in the late 1970s as a means of focusing attention on the need for quality of care. Although there has never been any national unanimity on these or other standards, the original list is a pointed reminder of the concerns of those who have been active in hospice care during its developmental phases.

The NHO standards were as follows:

1. The hospice program complies with applicable local, state, and federal law and regulation governing the organization and delivery of health care to patients and families.
2. The hospice program provides a continuum of inpatient and home care services through an integrated administrative structure.
3. The home care services are available twenty-four hours a day, seven days a week.
4. The patient/family is the unit of care.
5. The hospice program has admission critera and procedures that reflect:

    A. the patient/family's desire and need for service,

B. physician participation,
C. diagnosis and prognosis.

The hospice program encourages family paticipation in patient care and provides support for them.

6. The hospice program seeks to identify, teach, coordinate, and supervise people to give care to patients who do not have a family member available.
7. The hospice program acknowledges that each patient/family has its own beliefs or value system, and is respectful of them.
8. Hospice care consists of a blending of professional and nonprofessional services, provided by an interdisciplinary team, including a medical director.
9. Staff support is an integral part of the hospice program.
10. Inservice training and continuing education are offered on a regular basis.
11. The goal of hospice care is to provide symptom control through appropriate palliative therapies.
12. Symptom control includes assessing and responding to the physical, emotional, social, and spiritual needs of the patient/family.
13. The hospice program provides bereavement services to survivors for at least one year.
14. There will be a quality assurance program that includes:

    A. evaluation of services,

B. regular chart audits,
C. organizational review.

15. The hospice program maintains accurate and current integrated records on all patients and families.

16. The hospice complies with all applicable state and federal regulations.

17. The hospice inpatient unit provides space for:

A. patient/family privacy,
B. visitation and viewing,
C. food preparation by the family.

LICENSURE

Were it not for state licensure laws and other regulatory mechanisms, almost any group of individuals could set themselves up in the "hospice business" in order to profit at the expense of those they serve. Connecticut was the first state to adopt formal licensing arrangements for hospice care; Florida was a close second.

In 1987 the NHO reported that twenty-four states plus the District of Columbia had adopted formal licensure laws or regulations. In the January 1987 issue of *NHO News* NHO listed the following states as those having passed licensure laws: Arkansas, Colorado, Connecticut, Florida, Georgia, Illinois, Indiana, Iowa, Kentucky, Massachusetts, Michigan, Minnesota, Mississippi, Missouri, Montana, Nevada, New Mexico, New York, North Carolina, North Dakota, Rhode Island, South Carolina, West Virginia, Wisconsin, plus the District of Columbia. In addition, Arizona, California, Maryland, Nebraska, Ohio, Oklahoma, and Vermont were planning licensure laws.

CERTIFICATION

Medicare hospice certification, under the Tax Equity and Fiscal Responsibility Act of 1982, is based on the following requirements:

1. In order to be certified the local hospice program must assume all costs of care relative to the terminal illness for as long as the patient lives, including any hospitalizations related to the illness.

2. The hospice must retain professional management responsibility for continuity of care, both in the home and in the inpatient setting. Inpatient care may be secured from another institution on a contractual basis, provided it has policies consistent with those of the hospice, abides by the plan of care developed by the hospice, and allows the hospice to train its personnel.

3. Core services (i.e., nursing, medical social services, physician services, and counseling services, including bereavement and dietary counseling) must routinely be directly provided by hospice employees. The hospice may use contracted staff only to supplement its own staff during peak periods. A physician, a registered nurse, a social worker, and a pastoral or other counselor must be employed by the hospice and function as an interdisciplinary team.

4. Oriented and trained volunteers must be used in administrative or direct patient care roles. The volunteer staff must provide care that, at a minimum, equals 5 percent of total patient care hours of all paid employees and contract staff.

5. The hospice must make reasonable efforts to arrange for visits of clergy to patients who request such visits and must advise patients of this opportunity.

6. If state or local law provides for licensure, the hospice must be licensed.

ACCREDITATION

The most widely respected and used health care accreditation program is that of the Joint Commission on the Accreditation of Hospitals (JCAH). JCAH provides a *voluntary* accreditation program for hospices, but since July 1985 all hospital-based programs have been required to participate in the JCAH process.

Accreditation, once achieved, assures consumers that quality care is provided and that hospice care is as valid in one state as in another. Accreditation also assures third-party payers, be they governmental agencies, insurance companies, or employee benefit departments of major corporations, that the care provided by a hospice meets the same type of standards that they have come to expect from hospitals, home health agencies, or other recognized bodies.

Both certification and accreditation lists change periodically. Up-to-date information may be secured from state hospice organizations, the NHO, the Health Care Finance Administration, the JCAH, and the Hospice Association of America.

INVOLVE THE AMERICAN CORPORATE COMMUNITY*

Looking at hospice from the perspective of the business world—and that's where I come from—it appears that the quality of care may be in danger of dilution even as the hospice movement in our country begins to spread. This danger may come from many quarters. I'll mention four. First, there is the danger of well meaning but inadequately prepared practitioners entering the field and altering the reputation of hospice care. Second, there is the danger of regulations setting parameters of care expressed as components with less attention to quality and quantity of these components. Third, there is the danger of the profit-taker, a charlatan, taking advantage of the movement. And most importantly, there is the danger of simply not being able to provide hospice care because one might not have the resources to support that care.

We should not allow hospice care to lose its flavor, to lessen the attention given to the sick, to weaken its support for families. We must support this concept of care, and by support I mean including it in the overall scheme of health care and as an equal partner with all well-established hospitals and home care agencies. Government should keep and should actively seek to maintain high standards of true hospice care, provide adequate reimbursement, and insure the availability of hospice care to all segments of our population. Private insurance should recognize this care and provide coverage which it doesn't do completely now.

And there is a need for the direct involvement of the American corporate community. The first thing the corporate community can do is to provide for hospice care in their employee insurance coverage. We should examine the experience of those companies, such as General Electric, which have pioneered in this area. And we should also provide private, direct support for hospice care.

THOMAS S. MURPHY,
Chairman and Chief Executive Officer,
Capital Cities Communications, Inc.

*From an address delivered at ceremonies marking the Tenth Anniversary of Hospice Care in the United States and the Presentation of the Ella T. Grasso Award of The Connecticut Hospice, June 11, 1984.

Licensure, Certification and Accreditation*

The interrelationships of licensure, certification, and accreditation can be seen as an architectural structure. Licensure standards are a foundation. They set a minimum standard on which a state bases its regulation of the delivery of hospice care. State law may require a higher standard of care than federal regulations demand. Therefore, state licensure standards in many cases take precedence over the federal Medicare eligibility requirements.

The Conditions of Participation for hospices, which have been developed [the Tax Equity and Fiscal Responsibility Act], require that a hospice be in compliance with applicable state and local licensure laws (where they exist) in order to be eligible for Medicare certification. Obtaining a hospice license, where a licensure scheme exists, is necessary to establish a hospice program's eligibility for participation in the Medicare program (hereinafter "certification"). This would entitle a hospice program to receive Medicare payments for the services it provides to Medicare beneficiaries.

Certification serves as a framework built on the foundation provided by a licensure document. In determining whether a hospice program qualifies for certification, the federal government examines how successfully the intent of the state licensure law is implemented through the program elements; the manner in which services are provided through clinical and administrative management; the methods by which quality is monitored and inservice training is conducted, and the nature of the physical plant operation. In the absence of state licensure, the federal government would utilize the federal hospice standards enumerated in the Conditions of Participation.

Certification and licensure are interrelated substantively in this way. They also interrelate procedurally because of the manner in which the federal and state agencies coordinate their efforts in conducting the licensure and certification processes for hospices. The Health Care Financing Administration (HCFA), a branch of the Department of Health and Human Services, bears responsibility for administering federal certification.

HCFA arranges for the state to conduct the Medicare certification survey concurrently with its own state licensure inspection. The state survey team completes both inspections and returns the survey findings to HCFA, which confers certification. Federal certification insures that a hospice will receive Medicare reimbursement for the services it renders. It may also assist a hospice in obtaining reimbursement from commercial insurers, such as Blue Cross, which may regard federal certification as an indication of the hospice program's merit.

Accreditation is the roof that can be built over the foundation laid by licensure and the framework constructed by certification. Accreditation as a hospice by the Joint Commission on the Accreditation of Hospitals (JCAH) would represent the last step in the process of building the program's credentials. The accreditation process can be, but is not necessarily, utilized as a mechanism for evaluating a program's eligibility to maintain its status as a licensed and certified program. At present, the relationship of hospice accreditation to hospice licensure and certification precludes a national accrediting body from functioning in this role. In contrast, acute care hospitals may choose to seek hospital accreditation from the JCAH which, if a state so agrees, can deem the hospital for the purpose of licensure to have undergone its annual licensure inspection. The Social Security Act of 1965 permits the JCAH hospital accreditation to automatically qualify a hospital for federal certification.†

When a hospital successfully completes its hospital accreditation, it is said to have acquired "deemed status." This means that the JCAH has determined that the hospital fulfills the Medicare certification requirements. A minority of states allow JCAH accreditation to replace annual state licensure inspections, but those states that permit accreditation and licensure to be thus coordinated do so with the intention that the accrediting survey effort not be duplicated by state officials. Because the JCAH accreditation is both voluntary and expensive, hospitals may choose to forego the JCAH process. These hospitals would then proceed through state and federal channels to obtain licensure and certification respectively. At present under TEFRA, hospice programs do not enjoy the option of utilizing accreditation to secure deemed status.

*From Rosemary J. Hurzeler, Evelyn Barnum, and John Abbott, "Hospice: The Beginning or the End? The Impact of TEFRA on Hospice Care in the United States," *Bridgeport Law Review* 5:69, 1983. Reprinted by permission.

†Social Security Act, 42 U.S.C. 1395bb (1976).

LEVEL OF HOSPICE NURSING CARE ESSENTIAL
TO PATIENTS/FAMILIES*

Hospitalization can be a disorienting time. Confronted by new surroundings, new faces, and new regimens to adjust to, patients often feel unsettled and alone.

When the prognosis is terminal illness, the issues to be addressed spiral beyond the physical. They encompass the complex range of human emotions, be they anger, denial, hopelessness, or fear.

It is not surprising that at The Connecticut Hospice, patients and families often develop deep bonds with the nursing staff. In an era of high-technology medical care, Hospice nurses embody a high degree of *human* technology.

The deep and lasting impact of their work is eloquently described in the reflections of Hospice family members: "Thank you for being there when I needed you the most," one family member wrote the staff. "Your compassionate caring and helping and watching with me during my husband's final moments made his peaceful death seem natural and right."

"Without Hospice's help, we never could have managed Mother's illness at home," another family wrote, "nor would we have been witness to her final words, 'I have no pain . . . I am contented . . . and I am comfortable.' "

And still another, "The very beauty of Hospice in action defies the mystery of death."

At Hospice, nurses blend highly specialized skills and a rigorous dedication to their work with a sensitive awareness of the physical and emotional needs that surround a terminal illness. Their unique contributions have made The Connecticut Hospice a leader in hospice care in the United States.

Medically directed, multifaceted care, given by a team of trained professionals and coordinated by the Hospice nurse, represents the very best our health care system can give the dying patient and his or her family.

*From 1984 annual report of The Connecticut Hospice. Used with permission.

It is a tribute to the quality of that care that 75 percent of those who are eligible to choose hospice care within our home care service area do so.

In its ten-year history The Connecticut Hospice has provided palliative and support services for nearly 6,000 patients in Connecticut and other states.

The task is challenging, and far more than a technical or methodical one. It demands recognition of the patient's psychological, spiritual, emotional, and physical needs; observation of family dynamics; and respect for cultural, ethnic, and religious differences.

Because of this, staffing is no casual consideration at The Connecticut Hospice. The ratio of nursing staff to patients is one to three, equivalent to an intensive care unit in an acute care hospital. The justification for this staffing is that Hospice *does* provide intensive care nursing, not through monitors and respirators or by means of procedures performed, but through people.

At Hospice a patient's care plan is individually designed and based on clinical assessment and careful documentation of symptoms. Patients who are critically ill and whose conditions are rapidly changing require constant attention and assessment. Proper staffing ratios assure quality patient care.

"One of the things our caregivers can give patients and families is time," says Dianne Rawson, R.N., Vice-President for Inpatient Care. Hospice nurses provide intensive "human" care nursing, and proper staffing ratios permit nurses to move at a pace that is compatible with meeting the patient's and family's needs.

The focus of the Hospice nursing process is on the patient and family. They are—together—one unit of care. No patient is assessed in isolation from his or her family. Family dynamics are as carefully assessed as other factors that impact on a patient's physical and mental well-being. Likewise, the nurse-client relationship is participatory and interdependent. Patients and their families retain a voice in the care plan; they give as well as receive care.

As the patient and family's personal link to the rest of the caregiving team, the Hospice nurse coordinates the many details of the caring process. A highly supportive environment allows questions about the illness, its progress, and treatment to be discussed freely and honestly.

Families need not only someone to listen to them, but also someone to interpret accurately and explain the changes in the patient. It takes time and patience to establish a level of trust. As the patient draws closer to death, time spent with the family increases. There must be time to confer with other team members to ensure that all the parameters that contribute to the patient's status are considered.

This is true whether the patient is cared for at home or in the inpatient units. Many people with a terminal illness want to remain at home, and Hospice strives to provide the most appropriate setting for care. Hospice home care nurses provide quality care in the patient's own environment.

Quality patient care is possible because of individualized programs developed by the home care team with the cooperation of the family, family physicians, community health agencies, and involved Hospice team members.

As in inpatient care, it is a task that requires constant assessment, support, and coordination to help patients pursue the goal of quality living. This coordinated approach allows patients to continue their lives at home whenever possible.

When home care becomes inappropriate, the inpatient programs provide a homelike environment for care. Inpatient functions as a backup for acute-level care to assist in the management of pain and other symptoms.

Since 1980 The Connecticut Hospice has been licensed by the state as a short-term hospital and certified by the U.S. Department of Health and Human Services as a hospital with a hospice-based home care program.

As with home care, the Hospice inpatient nurse coordinates a team of interdisciplinary caregivers, including nurses, physicians, social workers, clergy, artists, pharmacists, and professional and lay volunteers.

Hospice nurses assist others in the learning process. They teach courses, lecture, and offer technical assistance to visitors, and provide training experiences for nursing students. And they continue to learn themselves. Their goal is not only to provide outstanding, compassionate care, but constantly to improve the quality of that care.

"Dying is a universal reality," Bess Bailey, R.N., Support Services Director, recently stated. "Hospice tries to do everything possible to make that final reality a dignified, worthy part of our total living."

Hospice nurses uphold the broadest definition of nursing as an art, a science, and a philosophy. Because of their energy, dedication, and professional skills, they uphold a tradition of quality patient care.

14

FUNDING PROBLEMS, RESOURCES, AND STRATEGY

The extent to which community leaders have been involved in the development of the hospice program will help to determine the success that will be experienced in securing financial support from the community. Hospice care is inherently highly visible. If corporate leaders, bankers, attorneys, educators, and other distinguished citizens are involved, approaches for funds will flow naturally. If the program has been developed without such participation, the enlisting of such people will help to facilitate funding.

FUNDING SOURCES

The following sources are listed as possibilities. The local fund-raising committee will think of others.

Foundations. The vast majority of private philanthropic foundations in the United States are small, family enterprises primarily oriented to a local community. Some of them operate with more formal procedures than others. Gifts are likely to be made to the causes in which the members of the distribution committee are personally interested.

Larger foundations tend to be highly organized, with formal procedures for application, review, reporting, and evaluation. Criteria for acceptance are

usually published and available for dissemination to interested parties.

The *Foundation Directory,* available in many public libraries, lists the larger foundations. Additional listings for those foundations located within a given state may be secured from state agencies, such as the office of the Secretary of the State, that regulate philanthropic giving.

All foundations are required to file reports of donations with the Internal Revenue Service (IRS). Such reports are public and may be secured by writing to any of the IRS district offices or one of the Foundation Center's ninety library collections.

United Way. Most United Ways require that a new organization become totally operative and must have carried on its activities for a period of time, before they consider it for membership. The nearest United Way office will be willing to provide information about the local procedures followed.

American Cancer Society. Because most hospice patients have cancer, it may be that the local or state unit of the American Cancer Society would be interested in helping to fund activities for the purpose of initiating hospice care.

Corporations. National corporations that offer the hospice benefit to their employees may be interested in helping to provide hospice care for those employees in areas where company plants or offices are located. Local corporations could be approached for start-up or continuing grants as well.

Individuals and families. As the hospice program grows, gifts, made in memory of patients cared for by the hospice unit, will increasingly help to support the program. Annual appeals, including sensitively prepared letters and descriptive materials, will offer substantive support. Direct personal solicitation of people who are known to have financial resources could be used to develop the starting impetus for the program.

Churches and other community groups. Local church budgets, especially in communities where the parishes are approached ecumenically for participation in a needed community service, should be considered not only for start-up costs, but for continuing support as well.

Service clubs are a viable means of support. One developing hospice received a $10,000 grant from the Rotary Club, which sponsored a community concert for the benefit of the hospice. All service clubs carry on activities that are designed to provide funding for causes of interest to the membership. (Offer a slide/speaking program to the club first to describe what hospice is and how the hospice program plans to implement it.)

A variety of community organizations—ethnic, religious, professional, public interest—sponsor such events as dances, concerts, walk-a-thons, marathons, and other sports events for programs with high visibility. Hospice care constitutes an ideal subject for such events.

Area agencies on aging. Area Agencies on Aging have, on occasion, funded hospice development, although the budgets of such programs currently may not be viable. Also, the agencies limit services rendered to senior citizens, thus excluding large portions of the population from care.

Legislative appropriations. One hospice program secured two legislative appropriations for the conduct of a feasibility study. Such political avenues are, however, relatively difficult to follow. But if the local hospice has board members or volunteers who are involved in state government, the avail-

ability of state surplus funds at the end of the fiscal year could be explored.

Hospital or Visiting Nurse Association budgets. Some hospice boards of directors, after careful consideration of the positive and negative factors associated with becoming an independent community organization, have sought—and received—inclusion of the program within the operating structures of hospitals, visiting nurse associations, or other health care institutions. The already existing organization then offers administrative, financial, reimbursement, volunteer service, public relations, and fund-raising services to the hospice portion of the total program.

Some hospice planners have rejected such opportunities because of loss of control of the hospice. Many hospitals and visiting nurse associations have themselves instituted plans for hospice care.

PROGRAMMATIC ASPECTS OF FUND-RAISING

As the hospice program develops, a variety of programmatic tools, when adequately publicized through a public relations program, will enhance the fund-raising capabilities of the hospice. A few possibilities are noted here.

Feasibility studies—often required for Certificate of Need applications or other regulatory processes—when publicized, may present a highly valid statement indicating the need for support.

Case statements are highly useful with foundations and corporate philanthropic committees.

Public forums and educational training sessions, often carried on by hospice experts from existing hospice programs, provide good opportunities for publicity. Many hospices have conducted day-long conferences for health care professionals or for civic leadership in the community.

Media events—presentations of awards, teas to honor well-known people, imaginative presentations of hospice—are highly useful in building a climate that will generate support.

15

PAYING THE BILL

The option of hospice care throughout the United States has become available to patients and families largely as the result of coverage of the costs of care by third-party payers. The principal sources of third-party coverage are Medicare, Blue Cross, private insurance companies, and Medicaid.

MEDICARE

In 1982 the U.S. Congress passed the Tax Equity and Fiscal Responsibility Act, which, for the first time, incorporated a hospice benefit providing for payment of hospice costs for Medicare recipients. Although a "sunset" provision called for review of the Act in 1986, the Congress voted to eliminate this provision, thus in effect extending such coverage indefinitely.

Out of 1,465 hospices in operation as of January 1, 1986,* only 245 have become certified, and thereby available to consumers with the Medicare benefit. Reasons for this are outlined on pages 62 and 64.

*1,568 hospices less 103 which are in planning stage.

Hospice Benefits Under Medicare†

What is hospice care? Under Medicare, hospice is primarily a comprehensive home care program which provides all the reasonable and necessary medical and support services for the management of a terminal illness, including pain control. Covered services include physician services, nursing care, medical appliances and supplies (including outpatient drugs for symptom management and pain relief), home health aide and homemaker services, therapies, medical social services, and counseling. In addition to the broad range of outpatient services, short-term inpatient care is also covered. When a patient receives these services from a Medicare-certified hospice, Medicare hospital insurance pays almost the entire cost. There are no deductibles or co-payments, except for limited cost-sharing for outpatient drugs and inpatient respite care.

Who is eligible? To be eligible for hospice care, four conditions must be met:

†Reprinted from Department of Health and Human Services, Health Care Financing Administration Publication No. HCFA 02154, January 1984.

1. the patient is eligible for Medicare (Part A) hospital insurance;
2. the patient's doctor and the hospice medical director certify that the patient has a terminal illness;
3. the patient signs a statement choosing hospice care instead of standard Medicare benefits for the terminal illness;
4. the patient receives care from a Medicare-certified hospice program.

Who can provide hospice care? Hospice services can be provided by a public agency or private organization that is primarily engaged in furnishing care to terminally ill people and their families. To receive Medicare payment, the agency or organization must be certified by Medicare to provide hospice services—even if it is already approved by Medicare to provide other kinds of health services.

How long can hospice care continue? Special benefit periods apply to hospice care. A patient can receive hospice care for two periods of 90 days each and one 30-day period—a lifetime maximum of 210 days. If hospice care is chosen for the terminal condition but later the patient decides not to use it, he or she can cancel at any time and resume standard hospital and medical insurance benefits under Medicare Part A and Part B. If cancellation is made before the end of a hospice period, any days left in that period are forfeited, but the patient is still eligible for any remaining hospice periods. For example: if a patient cancels at the end of 60 days in the first 90-day period, he or she loses the remaining 30 days. However, the patient is still eligible at a future time for the second 90-day period and one 30-day period. A patient can change from one hospice program to another once during each period without canceling the hospice care.

If a patient continues to need services after the hospice benefit periods are exhausted, the hospice must continue providing care unless the patient no longer wants hospice services.

How is payment made? Medicare pays the hospice directly for the full cost of all the reasonable and necessary covered services it provides for a terminal illness and related health problems. There are no deductibles or co-payments, except for two items:

1. Drugs or biologicals for pain relief and symptom management. The hospice can charge 5% of the reasonable cost, up to a maximum of $5, for each outpatient prescription for pain relief and symptom management.
2. Inpatient respite care. During a hospice period a patient may need short-term inpatient care to enable the person who regularly assists to get some temporary relief. This is called *respite care* for which the hospice can charge 5% of the cost of the inpatient stay, up to a total of $356 (1984 amount). The patient may not be charged more than this amount during a period that begins when a hospice plan is first chosen and ends 14 days after such care is canceled. (Respite care is limited each time to stays of no more than five days in a row.)

Are other Medicare benefits available in addition to hospice care? Since Medicare hospital insurance (Part A) covers the full cost of all medical and support services for a terminal condition, the patient gives up the right to payment for standard Medicare benefits for the terminal illness when hospice care is chosen. However, there are two exceptions: (1) If a patient's attending physician is not working for the hospice, Medicare medical insurance (Part B) continues to pay for his or her services in the same way it usually pays for other doctors' services. Medicare pays for 80% of the approved amount for covered services after the annual Part B deductible is met. (2) Medicare continues to cover treatment for conditions other than the terminal illness, under standard Medicare benefits. All other services must be provided by or through the hospice. When care from a hospice is chosen, Medicare cannot pay for treatment for the terminal illness which is not for symptom management and pain control; care provided by any other hospice (unless the patient's hospice arranged it); care from another provider which is the same as, or duplicates, care the hospice is required to provide.

WHAT HAPPENS TO MEDICARE PATIENTS IF A HOSPICE IS NOT CERTIFIED?

Under certain circumstances Medicare will pay for some kinds of hospice care. The following table

Medicare Reimbursement Differences

SERVICES RENDERED	MEDICARE HOME CARE	HOSPICE HOME CARE
Skilled nursing	Per need	Per need
Home health aide	80 hours/month	Per need
Drugs	No (riders or additional coverage needed)	For palliative care related to terminal illness only (5% co-pay)
Medical supplies/ equipment	Per need (80%)	Per Need Related to terminal illness only
Medical social work	Per need	Per Need
Therapies (physical, occupational)	Per need	Per Need
Hospitalizations	Deductible and coinsurance apply (additional coverage needed)	Related to terminal illness only (needs control)

outlines Medicare coverage under both the hospice benefit and its regular coverage.

BLUE CROSS

There are some seventy-seven Blue Cross companies throughout the United States. Each company serves two kinds of subscribers: those who are covered under national plans sponsored by large corporations with employees at a number of locations in different states, and those who are covered through the local or area firm that they work for. Each subscriber, in turn, has the coverage that has been arranged by his or her own employer, so that even if the company has a hospice benefit, that coverage may not have been bought by any individual employer.

Fifty-nine Blue Cross plans, out of the seventy-seven plans, offer a hospice benefit for *local* accounts.

The Blue Cross and Blue Shield Association has issued a recommended plan for its member groups to use for their *national* benefit accounts. This document ("Contract Language" and list of exclusions and limitations), quoted below, will be useful in checking with Blue Cross and Blue Shield in a particular state in order to determine the details of the coverage they offer to both national and local accounts.

Contract Language

Services provided by a hospice program for care of a terminally ill member with a life expectancy of six months or less. The services must be provided according to a physician-prescribed treatment plan.

1. Professional nursing services of an RN, LPN or LVN
2. Home health aide services
3. Medical care rendered by hospice care program physician
4. Therapy services except dialysis treatments
5. Diagnostic services
6. Medical and surgical supplies and durable medical equipment
7. Prescribed drugs
8. Oxygen and its administration
9. Medical social services
10. Respite care
11. Family counseling related to the member's terminal condition
12. Dietitian services
13. Inpatient room, board and general nursing service

The model plan has the following "Hospice Care Exclusions and Limitations."

----

1. No hospice care benefits will be provided for:
   A. Medical care rendered by the patient's private physician
   B. Volunteer services
   C. Pastoral services
   D. Homemaker services
   E. Food or home-delivered meals
   F. Private-duty nursing services
   G. Inpatient services
   H. Inpatient services except for respite care. (Inpatient care is usually covered under a subscriber's regular hospitalization plan.)
2. Respite care benefits are limited to a maximum of _____ days.
3. Respite care benefits are limited to _____ days every _____ months.

Note that bereavement care is not covered in the model plan for national accounts. Blue Cross explains that this is due to the tremendous variation in bereavement services available in different sections of the United States. (Bereavement care, as pointed out in chapters 6 and 7, is essential whether or not paid for by Blue Cross. If the effort is a volunteer one, response to such lack of coverage will differ considerably from a situation in which it is a service by paid professionals.)

MEDICAID

Medicaid reimbursement for hospice services was approved by the U.S. Congress on March 20, 1986, as part of a mammoth Budget Reconciliation Act. For the first time the states were permitted to reimburse for hospice care services under the Medicaid program.

Under this provision hospice care may be provided to a patient who is a resident of a skilled nursing facility or an intermediate-care facility.

INSURANCE COMPANIES

Many employees are covered through major medical or other health insurance coverage as part of employee benefit plans. Insurance companies offer such plans to employers who subscribe to them and, in some instances, to individual subscribers.

As of January 1987 mandatory insurance coverage of hospice care is provided for in Arizona, Colorado, Michigan, New York, and Washington.

During the preparation of this manual, major insurance companies were asked to describe their hospice benefits so that the information could be made available to local churches. The table on page 73 shows the results of this research.

AGE VARIATIONS

If hospice care is to be paid for appropriately, it is of paramount concern to analyze what is available by age. The following table indicates the variations, for example, between a sixty-four-year-old patient and one who is sixty-five (see page 73).

Health maintenance organizations (HMOs) in some local communities may provide hospice coverage, but there is no national uniformity of practice in this regard. Individual HMOs should be contacted to determine or make local arrangements.

CORPORATIONS

The General Electric Company was the first major American corporation to offer a hospice benefit to its employees (see chapter 16). The International Union of Electrical, Radio, and Machine Workers and the United Electrical, Radio, and Machine Workers were very much involved in the negotiations for this coverage, which began on January 1, 1980. Westinghouse and RCA soon followed suit. American Can, Capital Cities Communications, and the United Technologies Corporation added a hospice benefit shortly. The Postal Workers Union also secured a hospice benefit for its members.

The results of a 1985 survey conducted by the Washington Business Group on Health showed

Insurance Coverage of Hospice Care

Insurance Company	Home Care	Inpatient Care	Bereavement
Aetna	$3,000 lifetime	30 days lifetime	No
American General	Yes	Yes	Yes
Bankers of Iowa	No general summary of hospice benefits is available.		
Blue Cross/ Blue Shield	59 of 77 plans offer coverage for local Blue Shield accounts. Has model plan for national accounts.		
Colonial	$50.00 a day for 60 days as part of cancer care policy	No	
Cigna	Yes	Yes	3 visits
CNA	Optional case management program incorporates hospice care. Coverage offered in states mandating such coverage.		
Equitable	Yes	Yes	12 visits
General American		30 days	Yes
Hartford Life	Yes	Yes	
John Hancock	Yes	Covered under hospital contract	Yes
Metropolitan	$3,000 maximum	$7,500 maximum	Yes
MONY Financial Services (formerly Mutual of N.Y.)	100%	100% of first $150 for 21 days and then regular rate	Yes
Mutual of Omaha	100 visits per year	$185 per day maximum	$250 maximum
New York Life	100 visits	31 days—physician may certify more	6 visits
Northwestern National	$7,500 maximum with additional inpatient maximum of 30 days at $200 per day lifetime		
Pacific Mutual	Yes	Yes	8 sessions
Paul Revere	Yes	Yes	
Provident Mutual	Yes	Yes	
Prudential	$2,000 maximum	$3,000 maximum	$200 maximum
Time Insurance	Yes—100%		
Travelers	Yes	Yes	15 visits
Union Central	$3,500 maximum for hospice care		
Union-Mutual	$3,000	60 days	Yes
Washington National	$1,500	30 days	$100

Age Variations in Third-Party Coverage

	If Patient Is Over 65 (52%–75% of Patients)		If Patient Is Under 65 (25%–48% of Patients)
	If Care is Available in Certified Hospice	If No Medicare-Certified Hospice Is Available	
Medicare	Specific coverages	Regular Medicare	Not applicable
Blue Cross			Specific coverages
Private Insurance	See table of insurance coverage, above.		
Medicaid	Requires state implementation of federal guidelines		
HMOs			

that out of 131 Fortune 500 corporations, 68, or 51.9%, offered a hospice benefit to current employees. An additional 18 had such a plan under consideration, bringing the total to 65.6%. Fifty-six companies of the 131 (42.7%) were offering coverage to retirees. An additional 22 had such coverage under consideration, bringing the total to 59.5%.

16

PRIVATE SECTOR PERSPECTIVES: HOSPICE CARE REIMBURSEMENT

C.S. Tsorvas*

January 1, 1980, marks the date on which the coverage for hospice care was added under the General Electric Comprehensive Medical Expense Insurance Plan. The comprehensive plan was introduced on November 1, 1955. The latter event is significant in understanding the background and culture that led General Electric to adopt hospice care as a reimbursable expense under its insurance plan.

The comprehensive plan design in 1955 broke away from the tradition of hospital-surgical coverage that currently prevailed. It provided coverage for a broad range of ambulatory medical services in addition to coverage for hospitalization and surgery. It was also one of the first plans to include reimbursement for prescribed drugs.

Many skeptics questioned the feasibility of offering anything more than hospital and surgical coverage; after all, those were measurable risks. But who could tell what would happen if people were encouraged to use appropriate ambulatory care—and be reimbursed for such expense.

How times have changed! We now witness the accelerated trend in favor of reducing inappropriate hospitalization and encouraging ambulatory surgery, as well as other forms of ambulatory and home care.

The encouragement of ambulatory care has been a key objective of the GE comprehensive plan. This may help to explain why we had an affinity for hospice care as a potential area of covered expense when we first examined that issue. Other major objectives of the GE health insurance program were significant influential factors in the consideration of hospice reimbursement and other design changes that have been made to manage health care costs better. Six major objectives are kept in mind when considering plan modifications:

1. To provide health insurance coverage that gives effective protection against catastrophic illness expenses
2. To encourage quality ambulatory care that is appropriate and cost-effective
3. To maintain affordable levels of employee cost sharing
4. To educate employees on the use of alternative delivery systems
5. To help employees become better informed consumers of health care and to maintain good health

*From an address delivered at the 1984 Annual Meeting, National Hospice Organization, Hartford, Connecticut.

6. To protect the plan against excessive charges, overutilization, or inappropriate use of facilities and services, and against waste and duplication in the delivery of health care services

At about the same time hospice care was introduced, a number of other changes in plan design, aimed at encouraging the use of cost-effective alternatives to hospitalization, were also initiated. Coverage for ambulatory surgical facilities was added in 1979, reimbursing employees in full, on the same basis as for inpatient care. In 1980 coverage for posthospital recovery in extended-care facilities was included—up to 120 days maximum. We also added coverage for home health care programs after a period of hospital confinement, and coverage for home care treatment of hemophiliacs and for hemodialysis.

The decision to introduce hospice coverage was arrived at after an evaluation of the managed-care concept embodied in hospice and the emphasis on home care. It also required acceptance of the concept that palliative care, organized and delivered through a team of professionals, volunteers, and family members, was an effective approach for the care of the terminally ill patient. It was determined that hospice deserved reimbursement, as a form of quality care that was consistent with our health insurance objective to provide effective protection against the expenses of a catastrophic illness and to encourage the use of ambulatory and home care when appropriate and compatible with quality care, which we all want for ourselves and our families. Hospice care embodied those principles without lessening the quality of care; in many respects care was enhanced through the supportive care that could be provided only by interested family members.

At GE's 1979 national union negotiations hospice coverage was discussed and negotiated with the International Union of Electrical, Radio and Machine Workers, the United Electrical, Radio, and Machine Workers, and other unions represented at GE. Hospice care became a covered expense on January 1, 1980.

Blue Cross of Massachusetts helped to develop the criteria for approval of hospice programs under the GE insurance plan. Connecticut General and Metropolitan Life also are currently involved in the administration of GE's health insurance plan in various geographical areas of the country, and therefore are also administering the hospice care provision of our plan.

Blue Cross and other carriers that serve GE evaluate the company's experience under the comprehensive medical expense insurance plan on an ongoing basis. Their studies, as well as many others that have been conducted by different organizations, confirm that reimbursement of hospice care is a cost-effective health care alternative.

The consulting firm of Towers, Perrin, Forster, and Crosby has rated hospice reimbursement as one of the more effective cost-containment techniques for companies to adopt. And studies show that an increasing number of companies have come to the same conclusion, as GE did in 1980, and have added hospice reimbursement under their insurance plans. Health Research Institute reports that 35 percent of more than 600 major companies that responded to a recent survey had adopted hospice coverage.

Perhaps a word or two should be added on the current health care environment as viewed by private industry, and how employers can be encouraged to become supportive of the hospice concept.

The name of the game for employers these days is health care management—not only the effort to contain costs, but also the management of health care in ways that contribute to better-quality health care, delivered and used cost-effectively. A companywide effort to achieve these goals that is under way within General Electric is strongly supported both at the corporate level and by local GE management. The same type of intensive effort to manage health care costs is under way in many companies.

I'll tell you a little about GE's program and then suggest ways in which people who are dedicated to the growth and development of hospice can help to achieve increasing support from the employer community.

The objective of the program is to manage better health care expenditures in a way that contributes to quality health care for employees, retirees, and their dependents, within affordable costs. More than 150 health care coordinators have been assigned responsibility for health care management for their business localities.

The health insurance plan designs encourage employees to use ambulatory care and other cost-effective medical care, including second surgical opinions, ambulatory surgical facilities, extended-care facilities, and home care, rather than continued hospitalization, and hospice care for the terminally ill.

Managers have been urged to participate in local business coalitions that are involved in health care management. In that way they can become knowledgeable about their local health care environment and develop practical approaches to make sure that cost-effective, quality health care is being provided.

The insurance carriers that are involved in processing medical claims are expected to analyze health care utilization data and take action to make sure that employees and the company are protected against paying excessive charges.

A major segment of the health care managment program is the area of employee education on health care and the emphasis being given throughout the company to wellness programs. These efforts include health fairs, communication programs, health risk appraisals, and other actions directed at maintaining good health.

Based on my knowledge of what other employers are doing in the health care management area, I think it is fair to say that there is a universal consensus as to the need for a data base that will permit detailed evaluation of health care expenditures and identification of abuses, such as excessive charges and inappropriate or unnecessary care. Putting it positively, the data will help to identify cost-effective, quality providers and to encourage employees to consider such providers when faced with the need for medical services.

As you may know, private industry and government targeted hospital expenditures in recent years as a high-priority area for cost-containment efforts. That was no surprise, considering that hospital benefits represent, for most employers, more than half of their health insurance costs, and hospital charges have been increasing each year at a rate much higher than the general cost of living.

Industry has attempted to monitor and make certain that hospital utilization was necessary through the use of hospital utilization review programs, which include precertification, concurrent review, and discharge planning programs. In addition, the government's change to a prospective reimbursement system for hospitals seems to have provided hospitals with an added incentive to become more efficient providers.

As the focus moves to other medical providers, hospice will come under the same scrutiny. There will be an increasing need for hospice to demon-strate that it is policing itself as a movement, to guard against abuses, excessive charges, and inappropriate care.

Effective accreditation standards and a continued consciousness of the need for careful management of health care expenditures are steps that hospice workers should keep in mind as they look to the future and the expectations of private industry.

Recently I came across a book titled *Home Care;* hospice was just one of the chapters in that book. The rest dealt with home care for long-term illness and how a family might consider the options available as to appropriate care

- if the patient is hospitalized;
- if the patient is in a sheltered-care facility;
- if the patient is at home; or
- if the patient is in a rehabilitation facility.

The book raised a question for me. I wondered if the lessons and experience of people dealing with the terminally ill, through the organized, managed care approach of hospice, could be applied to long-term care cases, or even cases in which home care could be used for recovery over a relatively short period.

Somehow I believe that the hospice concept as applied to the terminally ill is just the beginning and that there is an opportunity for the same principles that have been applied by hospice to be used in other types of cases. I'm referring to effective case management, a coordinated team approach of professionals whose objective is to develop a treatment program that is the most appropriate for the patient's condition—in cases that involve long-term care—for example, of stroke victims, of comatose patients, of patients with degenerative brain or muscle conditions, of paraplegics. For those who are involved with health care issues these are interesting questions and challenging times. They call for a cooperative effort on the part of all sectors of society, both private and public, to arrive at workable, practical approaches that contribute to more cost-effective delivery and use of health care.

I offer a few suggestions related to employers' expectations about hospice and health care. Hospice care exemplifies the type of organized managed care that already has strong support among employers; that support can be further strengthened through more evaluative information as to the utilization and cost of hospice care compared with other types of hospital and medical treatment.

Keeping employers well informed about hospice activities and effectiveness in treating the terminally ill can go a long way to building an even larger base of employer support for the hospice concept.

17

COMMUNITY ASSESSMENT

The American Cancer Society (ACS) statistics for states that appear in chapter 3 will be helpful in determining the number of cancer cases in the local community and relationship between the overall averages. Current cancer statistics may be secured from a local branch of the ACS, from state health department officials responsible for morbidity statistics, or from health departments or planning agencies.

Likewise, ACS statistics will be helpful in projecting what the situation will probably be in the immediate future. To this end the ACS publishes "How to Estimate Cancer Statistics Locally," a formula for local use. It should be used with caution.

Local community cancer statistics should be supplemented by available estimates of deaths from terminal illnesses other than cancer. However, most hospice programs find that cancer patients account for 90 to 95 percent of their case load.

Once some information is available on current or prospective need, the local committee will want to determine its options for care in the community.

How to Estimate Cancer Statistics Locally

Community Population	Estimated No. Who are Alive, Saved from Cancer	Estimated No. Cancer Cases Under Medical Care in 1986	Estimated No. Who Will Die of Cancer in 1986	Estimated No. of New Cases in 1986	Estimated No. Who Will be Saved from Cancer in 1986	Estimated No. Who Will Eventually Develop Cancer	Estimated No. Who Will Die of Cancer If Current Rates Continue
1,000	10	5	1	3	1	280	180
2,000	20	11	4	7	3	560	360
3,000	30	16	5	10	4	840	540
4,000	40	21	7	13	5	1,120	720
5,000	50	26	9	16	6	1,400	900
10,000	100	52	18	33	12	2,800	1,800
25,000	250	131	45	79	30	7,000	4,500
50,000	500	162	90	158	59	14,000	9,000
100,000	1,000	525	180	325	122	28,000	18,000
200,000	2,000	1,050	360	650	244	56,000	36,000
500,000	5,000	2,625	900	1,575	590	140,000	90,000

NOTE: The figures are only a rough approximation of actual data for your community and should be used with caution. Every effort should be made to obtain actual data from a registry source. Reprinted by permission of American Cancer Society® from 1986 *Cancer Facts and Figures.*

Are there hospice programs in operation? Whom do they serve? Where are they located? What other programs are serving the dying population? Do local or regional hospitals have separate units for cancer patients? What services are offered by public health nursing agencies to the same patient population? Are services being offered by private-duty nursing agencies, perhaps operated from a proprietary or profit-making base? And what kind of services are offered?

CONSUMER OPERATIONS

The *Checklist for Consumers*, which appears at the back of this manual, was prepared by the National Consumers League and contains questions that will be useful in evaluating the quality of services being offered to the terminally ill population.

Special attention should be given to the extent to which family members are being served along with the patients. Family care constitutes the ever necessary base on which all programs should be judged.

REIMBURSEMENT QUESTIONS

If a local hospice program is experiencing reimbursement problems, it will be helpful to isolate each aspect of the problem by seeking answers to the following questions: What coverage is available for hospice care? Is the hospice program certified by Medicare? If not, why not?

If coverage is not available to people in the community, at what level is the decision being made? Is it a federal issue through Medicare or Medicaid? Is it a state issue? Does the presence or absence of Blue Cross reimbursement affect the matter? Do local employers provide hospice benefits for their employees? If not, at what level is that decision made and could the church influence it?

PHYSICIAN QUESTIONS

To what extent are local physicians supportive of hospice? Are they involved in the hospice program itself? Are there ways in which the church could influence their participation?

PAY A VISIT

The committee may want to visit the administrative and caregiving officials involved to get their perspective on the whole situation. Such a visit—if carried on with an opening inquiry as to how the committee can best serve as a hospice advocate—will greatly enhance the sense of communication within the community.

BE ECUMENICAL

Whenever possible, if several parishes work together on the task, the process will lead toward a more broadly based community endeavor. And patients and their families will be better served.

18

AGENDA FOR THE FUTURE*

Hospice care is too new to survive without a struggle. The traditional medical establishment has been challenged on principle to provide for comfort instead of perpetuating curative measures that may, indeed, be more financially profitable. At the same time governmental health and welfare programs have been seriously affected by the Graham-Rudmann era, which began in 1986.

Some hospice programs that were established in the late '70s and early '80s as a quick response to desires by health care professionals and citizens alike to provide more humane care have ceased to exist. Other programs are being established, especially since the U.S. Congress removed the sunset provision and made the hospice benefit a permanent part of the Medicare program. *Virtually every hospice program is beset by fiscal problems.*

Because of the complexities of the issues and the interrelationships of hospice care with other components of the health care system, the continuation of hospice care requires a new era of citizen advocacy based on study of the facts, formation of coalitions of like-minded groups, and a hard look into the future.

A number of major issues are, and will continue to be, crucial for hospice care. Opinions on these topics vary widely. Church-related educational and advocacy programs need to consider the many ramifications of each topic.

*Material in this chapter is taken from private correspondence between the editor and the people named.

PRIORITY OF CARE FOR THE DYING

Perhaps the most fundamental question relates to the priority given to the right of every American to live as fully and completely as possible for as long as life lasts. The hospice philosophy is based on a conviction that the "right to life, liberty and pursuit of happiness" continues until the very end. Governmental, educational, and health care programs give far more prominence to birth than to death. If life is a journey from start to finish, then the end of the pilgrimage requires far more emphasis than American society has given it in the past.

QUALITY OF CARE

Rosemary J. Hurzeler, President of The Connecticut Hospice, identifies the need for quality care as one of the major issues that affects the future of hospice. She looks to the day when the accreditation of a hospice program by the Joint Commission on the Accreditation of Hospitals (JCAH) will carry the same universally respected and accepted sign of approval as does JCAH accreditation of a hospital. She points out, however, that hospice quality cannot be left solely to the accreditation process. It requires the firm and unequivocal determination of every hospice in the nation, as well as every citizen advocacy group concerned about hospice, to make sure that no patient is denied quality of life because a hospice program fails to carry out the principles of quality of care.

From this standpoint, Claire Tehan, Vice-President for Hospice of the Hospital Home Health Agency of California, notes that data from a JCAH survey show "that those Hospice program characteristics which distinguish hospice from other terminal care are not always provided; bereavement follow-up, interdisciplinary care and spiritual support are not up to standard. Under such circumstances, people who have every right to expect quality are not receiving it."

REIMBURSEMENT—WHAT IS THE GOVERNMENT'S ROLE?

Opinions vary widely on questions related to the extent of publicly funded reimbursement mechanisms in paying the cost of hospice care. Attention has been focused on congressional action, including the hospice benefit within the Medicare program, because, on a national basis, most hospice patients are Medicare beneficiaries.

Two kinds of issues center around the hospice benefit: what it does include and what it does not include. Its proponents point out that whereas traditional Medicare was established from a provider perspective, the hospice benefit was consumer oriented. The act was created in such a way as to encourage quality of care, to insist that hospices maintain management control of the care being provided, and to prevent "post office-box hospices" from being established merely to capture funding at the consumers' expense. With the permanence of the benefit, advocates of the plan are confident that many more hospices will become certified than in the past.

Critics of the program believe that hospice benefit rules and regulations prevent most hospice programs from applying for certification. They think that the fact that a small, inadequately financed hospice must assume all costs related to the terminal illness for a Medicare patient for as long as he or she lives is a deterrent to participation. Many home care hospices, especially in small towns and rural areas, have had difficulty negotiating inpatient contracts and employing their own nurses. The latter has caused many groups to favor a waiver of some rules and regulations governing hospice programming.

Philip G. DiSorbo, Executive Director of the Hospice of Schenectady, New York, comments that "we are only getting 70% of costs reimbursed; public pressure must be kept on hopefully to increase this but at least to prevent its erosion." Stating that current Medicare regulations make hospice care too restrictive, he indicates the need to serve more people. Claire Tehan, in urging a change in the Medicare benefit, would prefer "a flat Hospice DRG payment."

Many hospices are seriously affected by lack of coverage for AIDS patients, rapidly progressive cancer patients under age sixty-five, and children. In order to qualify for Medicare disability, adults must have been disabled for two years; many cancer patients die too quickly to take advantage of such coverage. National Hospice Organization leaders point out that recent legislation providing for hospice coverage within Medicaid has made it possible for many others, including AIDS patients, to be cared for within hospice programs. But the fact remains that up to a third of hospice patients are too young for Medicare, and insufficient attention has been devoted to them.

What *is* the role of government in financing hospice care? This question is open for discussion and debate, and clearly those who develop an advocacy role are in a strong position to help influence the outcome.

MORE INSURANCE COVERAGE NEEDED

There is a need for far more advocacy within the insurance industry, on one hand, and the state legislatures, which pass laws controlling insurance coverage, on the other. Broad coalitions of all those who are involved in insurance matters need to be framed to mandate hospice coverages according to state law. Carol E. Dixon, R.N., M.S., director of clinical services of the Hospice of Dayton, identifies the "development of consistency and adequacy of insurance coverage throughout industry and insurance companies" as essential.

INFORMING THE PUBLIC

Issues relating to public awareness of hospice care are crucial to the future. Tehan reports that the general "squeeze" on health care has had a definite effect on hospice. "There is tremendous need," she says, "for people to know about Hospice and to understand that it is an alternative to senseless treatments when there is no longer any hope of cure. It is essential for the public to know when and how to ask their physician for hospice care."

William E. Gillis, Administrator of Clover Health Care in Auburn, Maine, says that the general public needs to know what is available in the community so that there will be a smooth transition from hospital to care in the home to inpatient hospice. Many hospice leaders cite the need for churches to join in sponsoring training and educational programs on death, dying, and loss. There is great appreciation for church leadership, which has led the way in this regard in the past.

BROADENING THE BASE

There is great concern surrounding questions related to broadening the base of those being served by hospice. Charlotte N. Shedd, R.N., M.N., Executive Director of the Hospice of Buffalo, calls attention to the need to ensure hospice services for the patient who does not have a primary care person. Her plan is to use the services of a "surrogate family," drawing participants from thirty congregations in the Buffalo area. Carol

Dixon discussses new methods of delivery care, such as day-care programs, and alternative residency for patients lacking a home.

INTEGRATION INTO THE SYSTEM

Hospice care needs to be integrated into the existing health care system. Paul Montgomery, Hospice Coordinator of Emerson Hospital in Concord, Massachusetts, urges local groups to "use their power as consumers to bring together and coordinate working relationships between hospitals, VNA's, health care personnel and hospices."

THE NATURE OF HOSPICE

The nature of hospice will continue to be debated in years to come. DiSorbo says that "we are part of the official health care system and must remain so *without* losing the deep spirituality, wholeness, and interdisciplinariness, use of volunteers and inclusion of bereavement care. The spirit of hospice must be nourished and kept alive."

The nurturing of that spirit is clearly important to all of us.

Selected Annotated Bibliography on Dying and Death

Prepared by Betsey Lewis

HOSPICE

Hamilton, Michael, and Helen Reid, eds. *A Hospice Handbook: A New Way to Care for the Dying*. Grand Rapids, MI: William B. Eerdmans, 1980.

Munley, Anne. *The Hospice Alternative: A New Context for Death and Dying*. New York: Basic Books, 1983.
A sociologist, Sister Anne uses strokes both broad and penetratingly detailed to describe the psychosocial nature of hospice. Notable hospice insights include the search for "synthesis"; spiritual support (patients, families, care-givers); future of hospice in the health care system. This could be the book to choose if you are using only one.

Stoddard, Sandol. *The Hospice Movement: A Better Way of Caring for the Dying*. New York: Vintage Books, 1978.
Narrative introduction to hospice, from fifth century B.C. origins to twentieth-century emergence as a "movement." What it is to be a "hospice person."

DYING AND DEATH

Becker, Ernest. *The Denial of Death*. New York: The Free Press, 1973.
Brilliant synthesis of thought in many fields on the role of death in human life. A work to grow with, bit by bit, over time. Pulitzer Prize winner.

Feifel, Herman, ed. *The Meaning of Death*. New York: McGraw-Hill, 1965.
Wide-ranging collection of commentaries (some outdated) about death—anthropology to religion, art to psychology. Practical table of contents facilitates selective use.

Grollman, Earl A., ed. *Explaining Death to Children*. Boston: Beacon Press, 1978.
Practical and sensitive guidance for parents. Chapters written by clergy and others.

Kastenbaum, Robert J. *Death, Society, and Human Experience*. St. Louis: C.V. Mosby, 1981.

Illuminating work, addressing "the interplay of life and death throughout all levels of our society." Especially useful index for repeated reference. Conclusions carefully documented.

Kubler-Ross, Elisabeth. *On Children and Death*. New York: Macmillan, 1983.
Author's long experience and special empathy for children is usefully concentrated for the benefit of parents who are losing or have lost a child. Also notable: chapter on "How Can Friends Help?" and an extensive bibliography.

———. *On Death and Dying*. New York: Macmillan, 1969.
Seminal work, now a classic in the field.

———, ed. *Death: The Final Stage of Growth*. Englewood Cliffs, NJ: Prentice-Hall, 1975.
Collection of commentaries (variable in quality) about dying and death.

Nouwen, Henri J.M. *The Wounded Healer: Ministry in Contemporary Society*. New York: Doubleday, 1972. Outstanding.

Slaikeu, Karl, and Steve Lawhead. *The Phoenix Factor: Surviving and Growing Through Personal Crisis*. Boston: Houghton Mifflin, 1985.
Detailed and realistic "plan for crisis resolution." Practical ideas for friends and other helping people. Interweaves compassion and professional insights through case histories. Personal and conversational style.

LOSS AND BEREAVEMENT

LeShan, Eda. *Learning to Say Good-by: When a Parent Dies*. New York: Macmillan, 1975.
Warm, understandable. Approximately grades 5 through 12.

Pincus, Lily. *Death and the Family: The Importance of Mourning*. New York: Vintage Books, 1976.
Compelling case for accepting loss, including its pain, toward renewed wholeness of life. Many examples. The single clearest book on bereavement. Immensely valuable.

Stearns, Ann Kaiser. *Living Through Personal Crisis.* Chicago: Thomas More Press, 1984.

Personal guidance through loss toward recovery. Direct and nontechnical language.

Tatelbaum, Judy. *The Courage to Grieve.* New York: Lippincott & Crowell, 1980.

A psychiatric social worker presents the grief experience from many angles. A hopeful thrust permeates the work. Authoritative, but not academic, in atmosphere.

Temes, Roberta. *Living with an Empty Chair: A Guide Through Grief.* New York: Irvington Publishers, 1980.

A small, "welcoming" little paperback, gently and affirmingly addressed to a widowed person. Also useful in a personal way to those who are helping widowed people. Illustrated with delicately facilitative photographs and line drawings.

PERSONAL EXPERIENCE

Albertson, Sandra Hayward. *Endings and Beginnings: A Harvesting.* New York: Random House, 1980.

Young author movingly describes her husband's brief terminal illness and his death. Involves tension between sensitivity and realism, pain and love. Wise concluding segment about bereavement.

Alsop, Stewart. *Stay of Execution: A Sort of Memoir.* Philadelphia: J.B. Lippincott, 1973.

Honesty, humor, vitality, unswerving engagement with living characterize this journalist/patient's "process of adjustment" in coming to terms with his own terminal illness—and come to terms he does in a memorable way. A strong book.

Bishop, Joseph P. *The Eye of the Storm.* Minneapolis: Bethany House, 1976.

With a particular gift for sharing experience, Bishop describes his and his wife's coping with tragedy and their eventual discovery that "the peace of God is . . . in the eye of the storm." Intimate. Inspiring.

Lewis. C.S. *A Grief Observed.* New York: Bantam Books, 1979.

A believer's candid journal of mind and spirit. Painful, yet also can be uniquely comforting to someone suffering a similar wrenching sorrow.

FICTION FOR CHILDREN

Fiction selected to suit the development of an individual child can be a fine aid toward appropriate awareness of death. There are favorites, old and new, such as: Kenneth Grahame, *The Wind in the Willows;* Doris Smith, *A Taste of Blackberries;* E.B. White, *Charlotte's Web;* and Margery Williams, *The Velveteen Rabbit.*

A helpful list of children's books is included in the bibliography of Elisabeth Kubler-Ross' book *On Children and Death.*

FICTION FOR ADULTS

Agee, James. *A Death in the Family.* New York: Bantam Books, 1971.

Intense and forceful writing conveys a sense of immediacy. Unforgettably depicts the acute and varied suffering of members of a family (including a little boy) on the sudden death of a young husband and father. Protective irrationality is vividly shown.

Guest, Judith. *Ordinary People.* New York: Viking Press, 1976.

Depiction of the human need to express grief. Simple language.

Wilder, Thornton. *Our Town: A Play in Three Acts.* (1938) New York: Harper & Row, 1985.

An old favorite, memorable to reread in the context of new concern for dying and death.

PROFESSIONAL MATERIAL

Aries, Philippe. *The Hour of Our Death.* New York: Alfred A. Knopf, 1981.

Monumental in scope, yet eminently readable. Aries' scholarship sweeps from the early Middle Ages to modern times, interpreting Western attitudes toward death in cultural contexts.

Gonda, Thomas Andrew, and John Edward Ruark. *Dying Dignified: The Health Care Professional's Guide to Care.* Menlo Park, CA: Addison-Wesley, 1984.

From their experience in caring for terminally ill patients, two California physicians suggest many ideas and techniques. Continuity provided through use of recurring clinical examples.

Lindemann, Eric. "Symptomatology and Management of Acute Grief," *American Journal of Psychiatry* 101 (September): 141–48, 1944.

Pioneering modern work on bereavement. A definitive study of the grief reactions of families of Coconut Grove fire victims.

Parkes, Colin Murray. *Bereavement: Studies of Grief in Adult Life.* New York: International Universities Press, 1973.

Scholarly, humane, durable. Case histories of London widows.

Rando, Therese A. *Grief, Dying, and Death: Clinical Interventions for Caregivers.* Champaign, IL: Research Press Company, 1984.

Comprehensive, meticulously professional; yet also enhanced by the reflective comments of this experienced clinical psychologist.

Schoenberg, Bernard; Arthur C. Carr; Austin H. Kutscher; David Peretz; Ivan K. Goldberg, eds. *Anticipatory Grief.* New York: Columbia University Press, 1974.

Addresses the nature of loss and grief, especially as they unfold when a death is expected. Suggested multidisciplinary intervention possibilities for the patient, family members, and caregivers.

Sharkey, Frances. *A Parting Gift.* New York: St. Martin's Press, 1982.

One physician's view of childhood dying. Particular concern with the matter of truth—to share or withhold it—as observed over many years of pediatric practice.

RELATED MATERIALS PUBLISHED BY THE PILGRIM PRESS

AIDS: Personal Stories in Pastoral Perspective
Earl E. Shelp, Ronald H. Sunderland, and Peter W.A. Mansell, M.D. 1986. Includes chapters on "AIDS and the

Church," "Medical Facts About AIDS," "Nurses, Social Workers, and Physicians," and "Pastoral Perspectives and Recommendations."

Popular "Looking Up Series" of 24-page booklets (partial listing):

John E. Biegert. 1979. *Looking up . . . While Lying Down.*

———. 1981. *When Death Has Touched Your Life.*

———. 1985. *Staying In . . .*

Lois A. Bloom. 1986. *Mourning, After Suicide.*

Geneva M. Butz. 1986. *Color Me Well* (coloring booklet with prayers for children).

Joan E. Hemenway. 1985. *Holding On . . . While Letting Go.*

Doris Stickney. 1982. *Water Bugs and Dragonflies: Explaining Death to Children.*

Resources for Study, Education, and Training

Children's Hospice International

1101 King Street, Suite 131, Alexandria, VA 22314. (703) 684-0330

Supports health care agencies that treat terminally ill children and their families; coordinates support systems for parents and siblings of children who are experiencing serious illness, or those who have encountered the sudden loss of a child. Acts as a clearinghouse and public relations agency. Publication and audiovisual list available.

Connecticut Hospice Institute for Education, Training and Research

61 Burban Drive, Branford, CT 06405. (203) 481-6231

Produces multimedia resources for instructing health care professionals and other hospice workers on hospice care. Offers *A Hospice Orientation Program,* which includes six videotapes and a 250-page Resource Guide, and *An Overview by Discipline,* which includes ten tapes and study guides. Publishes policy and procedure manuals and produces other films. Also offers technical assistance and conducts an annual Week of Courses. Further information available.

Hospice Association of America

214 Massachusetts Ave., N.E., Suite 240, Washington, DC 20002. (202) 547-5263

Seeks to act as unified voice that represents all hospice providers without preferential treatment for any one organizational model. Acts as advocate on hospice issues and works for national legislation serving hospices. Established by the National Association for Home Care and the Association of Community Cancer Centers.

National Consumers League

600 Maryland Avenue, S.W., Suite 202 West, Washington, DC 20024.

Publishes *A Consumer Guide to Hospice Care.*

National Hospice Organization

1901 North Fort Myers Drive, Suite 402, Arlington, VA 22209. (703) 243-5900.

The only independent national organization devoted exclusively to hospice care in America. Through a wide range of advocacy programs promotes quality standards. Offers publications, technical assistance, and national and regional conferences. List of materials available on request.

Checklist for Consumers*

The following list of questions is intended to help a patient and family review hospice care.

QUESTIONS FOR PATIENT AND FAMILY

1. Have you discussed your condition with your doctor? What does the doctor think about continuing the treatment you have been receiving?

2. Have you decided, after talking to the doctor and to your family, that you want to forego further surgery or chemotherapy?

3. Have you and your family discussed the various options open to you?

4. If you remain at home, how will day-to-day care be managed?

5. Is 24-hour care going to be necessary in your situation? If so, can you and your family arrange for such care?

6. If the family assumes responsibility for care, are there other relatives and friends who can help?

7. If there is no relative or close friend who can be primary caregiver, would you want to be in a hospice program within a hospital or nursing home?

QUESTIONS ABOUT THE HOSPICE

1. Who are the people from the hospice who will be seeing you? Are they on the hospice staff, are they volunteers, or does the hospice contract for their services?

2. What will be your doctor's role in the hospice program? Will the hospice be talking to your doctor?

3. How often will you be seeing a hospice doctor?

4. Are nurses available 24 hours a day?

*Reprinted with permission from *A Consumer Guide to Hospice Care,* published by National Consumers League, February 1985.

5. What kind of training do the nurses have in treating the dying?

6. How often will a nurse visit you in your home?

7. Is there someone from the hospice to help you with your insurance forms? With financial problems or questions?

8. What if a member of your family has a problem with your care or a personal problem? What kind of help can the hospice provide?

9. Is there any kind of follow-up with your family?

10. Does the hospice have volunteers who can help your family with your care? What kind of training have they had?

11. What happens if there is a crisis in the middle of the night? Who takes calls after business hours—an answering service or member of the staff? If it's an answering service, how will your call be handled? Who will come to the house?

12. If you have to go back into the hospital, will you go to the hospital you were in before, or one associated with the hospice? Do you have any choice about hospitals?

13. What kind of follow-up does the hospice provide if you go into a hospital? Do they stay in touch, and if so, how?

COSTS

1. Will the hospice accept you whether or not you are covered by private insurance or Medicare or can pay your own bills?

2. Are there fees, and if so, how are they applied—per day, per visit, or on what other basis? Does the hospice have a payment plan?

3. If you can afford to meet a share of your costs, what will you be billed for?

4. Will the hospice handle the billing with Medicare or private insurance carriers?

5. Will the hospice negotiate for you with an insurance carrier if the carrier denies any charges?

PROGRAM

1. Does the hospice program mainly involve home care? If so, how will the hospice arrange for you to go into a hospital if

necessary? Does the hospice have its own facility with beds?

2. If the hospice is in a hospital or other institution, does it have a home care program as well? Is there a separate unit in the hospital or nursing home for hospice patients? Do the people who take care of you in the hospital follow up with your care if you go home?

STANDARDS

1. Does the hospice have state approval, where applicable, and if so, for what services?

2. Does the hospice have any kind of outside review? If so, by whom?

3. What kind of accreditation does the hospice have?